D1196947

THE TRIAL

a film by

Orson Welles

English translation and description of action
by Nicholas Fry

Simon and Schuster, New York

General Editor: Sandra Wake

SBN 671-20620-6
Library of Congress Catalog Card Number: 75-119353

Manufactured in Great Britain by Villiers Publications Ltd,
London NW5

CONTENTS

A NOTE ON THIS EDITION

The Trial was made originally with English dialogue and dubbed into French for its world premiere in Paris in 1962. The present publication is based on the French script published by *l'Avant-Scène du Cinéma*, which was itself based on Orson Welles's original script and supplemented by material obtained from a shot-by-shot viewing of the film. This version was translated into English and combined with a transcript of the English dialogue. The result was then finally checked against a print of the film obtained from the English distributor, in order to make it as accurate a rendering as possible of the film which the English or American spectator will see on the screen.

Sections which occurred in the original script but were either not shot or cut in the editing are indicated by square brackets in the text.

Acknowledgments and thanks are due to *l'Avant-Scène du Cinéma* for providing stills, and to Connoisseur Films Ltd., for supplying a print of the film.

ORSON WELLES ON *THE TRIAL*

Q : *In* The Trial, *you seem to be making a severe criticism of the abuse of power; or perhaps it's something more profound — Perkins appears as a kind of Prometheus* ...

WELLES : He's also a little bureaucrat. I consider him guilty.

Q : *Why do you say he's guilty?*

WELLES : He belongs to something which represents evil and which is a part of him at the same time. He is not guilty of what he's accused of, but he's guilty all the same : he belongs to a guilty society, he collaborates with it. But I'm not a Kafka analyst.

Q : *Should Joseph K fight?*

WELLES : He doesn't; perhaps he should, but I don't take sides in my film. K collaborates all the time. He does it in Kafka's book too. All I allow him to do is to defy the executioners at the end.

Q : *There is a version of the scenario with a different ending, where K is stabbed to death by his executioners.*

WELLES : I don't like that ending. To me it's a ' ballet ' written by a Jewish intellectual before the advent of Hitler. Kafka wouldn't have put that after the death of six million Jews. It all seems very much pre-Auschwitz to me. I don't mean that my ending was a particularly good one, but it was the only possible solution. I had to step up the pace, if only for a few moments ...

Q : *There is a fundamental change in the transposition of* The Trial *to the cinema. In Kafka's book, K is more passive than in the film.*

WELLES : I made him more active in the proper sense of the word. I do not think there is any place for passive characters in a drama. I have nothing against Antonioni, for instance, but in order to interest me, the characters must do something, from a dramatic point of view, that is.

Q : *Was* The Trial *an old idea of yours?*

WELLES : I once said that a good film could be made out of it, but I was not thinking of myself. A man came to see me and said that he thought he could raise the money for me to make a film in France. He gave me a list of films to choose from. And from this list of fifteen films I chose what I thought was the best; that was *The Trial*. Since I couldn't do a story I had written myself, I chose Kafka . . .

Q : *In* The Trial, *is the long tracking shot of Katina Paxinou* dragging the trunk while Anthony Perkins talks to her intended as a homage to Brecht?*

WELLES : I didn't see it that way. There was a long scene with her which lasted ten minutes, and which I cut anyway the day before the premiere in Paris. I only saw the complete film once. We were still doing the mixing and then suddenly the premiere was upon us. At the last moment I shortened the ten-minute scene. It should have been the best scene in the film, but it wasn't. Something went wrong, I guess. I don't know why, but it just didn't come out right. The subject of this scene was free will. It was tinged with black comedy and that was my main weapon. As you know it is always directed against the machine in favour of freedom.

Q : *When Joseph K sees the slides at the end of the film, with the story about the guard and the gateway etc., does this represent your own reflections on the cinema?*

WELLES : It was more a question of the technical problem involved in telling that story : if it was told at that point, the public would go to sleep; that is why I tell it at the beginning and only refer back to it at the end. The effect is the same as if it had been told at that point, and that way I was able to do it in a few seconds. But in any case the Advocate was not me.

Q : *A critic who greatly admires your work has said that in* The Trial *you repeated yourself* . . .

WELLES : . . . I do not repeat myself intentionally, but in my work there must certainly be references to what I have done in the past. Say what you like, but *The Trial* is the best film I ever made. One only repeats oneself when one is tired, and I was not tired. I have never been so happy as when I was making that film.

Q : *How did you shoot the long running sequence with Anthony Perkins?*

WELLES : We had a very long platform and the camera was

---

* The *Cahiers* interviewer would seem to be mistaken, since it is Miss Pittl, played by Suzanne Flon, who appears in the sequence with the trunk. However, Welles does not pick him up on this.

mounted on a wheel chair.

Q : *But it's incredibly fast!*

WELLES : Yes, but I had a Yugoslavian runner to push the camera.

Q : *One of the most remarkable things in your work is the constant effort to find solutions to the problems of directing ...*

WELLES : The cinema is still very young and it would be quite ridiculous if one couldn't find new things for it. If only I could make more films. You know what happened with *The Trial*? We were due to leave Paris for Yugoslavia in two weeks when we were told that we wouldn't be able to put up a single set there because the producer had already made another film in Yugoslavia and hadn't paid his debts. That's why we had to use that abandoned station. I had planned to make a completely different film. Everything was improvised at the last moment, because the whole physical concept of my film was quite different. It was based on the absence of sets. And the gigantic nature of the sets, which people have objected to, is partly due to the fact that the only setting I had was that old abandoned station. An empty railway station is vast. In the production as I originally envisaged it, the sets were to gradually disappear. The number of realistic elements was to gradually diminish, and to be seen to diminish by the spectators, until only open space remained, as if everything had been dissolved away.

Q : *The combined movement of the actors and the camera is very beautiful in your films.*

WELLES : That's a visual obsession. Thinking of my films, I feel that they are based not so much on a pursuit as on a search ...

In the cinema there should always be a process of discovery. I think that the cinema should be essentially poetic, which is why, not during the phase of preparation but during the shooting, I try to involve myself in a poetic process which is distinct from the narrative process or the dramatic process. But I am really a man of ideas; yes, above all else; I guess I am even more of a man of ideas than a moralist.

Cahiers du Cinéma
No. 165, April 1965

CREDITS:

Scenario and dialogue by	Orson Welles, based on the novel by Franz Kafka
Directed by	Orson Welles
Produced by	Alexander and Michael Salkind
Production companies	Paris Europa Productions (Paris), Hisa-Films (Munich), FI-C-IT (Rome)
Music composed and arranged by	Jean Ledrut
Musical leitmotif	The *Adagio* by Albinoni
Production director	Robert Florat
Assistants to the director	Marc Maurette, Paul Seban
Director of photography	Edmond Richard
Cameraman	Adolphe Charlet
Assistants	Max Dulac, Robert Fraisse
Stills photographer	Roger Corbeau
Art director	Jean Mandaroux
Assistants	Jacques d'Ovidio, Jacques Brizzio, Pierre Tyberghien, Jean Bourlier
Exterior settings	Guy Maugin
Editor	Yvonne Martin
Assistants	Chantal Delattre, Gérard Pollican
Special effects editor	Denise Baby
Sound engineer	Guy Villette
Assistants	Loiseau, Guy Maillet
Sound mixer	Jacques Lebreton
Assistant to the producers	Paul Laffargue
Administration by	Henry Dutrannoy
Production manager	Jacques Pignier
Assistants	Emile Blonde, Philippe Dubail
Continuity	Marie-José Kling
Make-up	Louis Dor
Wardrobe	Helène Thibault
Dressers	Mme. Brunet, Claudie Thary
Pin-screen images	A. Alexeieff and Claire Parker
Locations, interior	Gare d'Orsay, Paris
exterior	Globus-Dubrava, Zagreb

Studio	Studio de Boulogne
Shooting	26th March to 5th June 1962
World premiere	21st December 1962, Paris
Running time	120 minutes
Process	Black and white

CAST:

Joseph K	Anthony Perkins
The Advocate	Orson Welles
Miss Burstner	Jeanne Moreau
Leni	Romy Schneider
Hilda	Elsa Martinelli
Bloch	Akim Tamiroff
Inspector A	Arnoldo Foa
Assistant Inspector 1	William Kearns
Assistant Inspector 2	Jess Hahn
Miss Pittl	Suzanne Flon
Mrs. Grubach	Madeleine Robinson
The Courtroom Guard	Wolfgang Reichmann
Bert, the Law Student	Thomas Holtzmann
Irmie	Maydra Shore
Uncle Max	Max Haufler
Titorelli	William Chappell
The Chief Clerk	Fernand Ledoux
The Deputy Manager	Maurice Teynac
The Priest	Michael Lonsdale
The Examining Magistrate	Max Buchsbaum
First Policeman	Jean-Claude Remoleux
Second Policeman	Raul Delfosse
The Man in Leather	Karl Studer

Also, in scenes cut from the final version:

The Scientist	Katina Paxinou
The Archivist	Van Doude

THE TRIAL

Loud music. Part of the credits come up in white letters on a black background.

[*Close-up of a slide projector. The lens lights up, blinding us, and the camera pans, following the beam to a white screen.*]

1. One of Alexeieff's pin-head images flips up on the screen. It is a still showing the open gate of a fortress, with a GUARD *standing on the right.*[1] *(Still on page 2) The voice of the* NARRATOR *is heard off.*

NARRATOR *off* : Before the law there stands a Guard . . .

2. A second still picture of a TRAMP *approaching the gateway.*

NARRATOR *off* : A Man comes from the country, begging admittance to the law.

3. A closer view of the GUARD *by the gateway, his hand raised.*

NARRATOR *off* : But the Guard cannot admit him.

4. A similar view of the MAN. *(Still on page 2)*

NARRATOR *off* : Can he hope to enter at a later time?

5. Resume on the GUARD.

NARRATOR *off* : ' That is possible,' says the Guard.

6. Resume on the MAN *peering through the gateway.*

NARRATOR *off* : The Man tries to peer through the entrance. He has been taught that the Law should be accessible to every man.

7. Close-up of the GUARD, *his hand raised.*

NARRATOR *off* : ' Do not attempt to enter without my permission,' says the Guard. ' I am very powerful, yet I am the least of all the Guards . . .

8. A closer shot, looking in through the gateway.

NARRATOR *off* : ' From hall to hall . . .

9. The gateway with another now visible beyond it.

NARRATOR *off* : '. . . door after door, each Guard is more powerful than the last.'

---

[1] The pictures created by A. Alexeieff which we see at the beginning and towards the end of the film are formed by the play of light and shadow on images formed in relief by pins stuck into a thick white cloth.

10. Resume on the gateway (as in 1), the GUARD *and the* MAN *in front of it. Effects of lighting and different seasons — rain and snow — dissolve in and out on the same picture.*

NARRATOR *off* : With the Guard's permission the Man sits down by the side of the door, and there he waits. For years he waits. Everything he has he gives away in the hope of bribing the Guard, who never fails to say to him : ' I take what you give me only so that you will not feel that you have left something undone.' Keeping his watch during the long years, the Man has learned to know even the fleas in the Guard's fur collar . . .

11. Close-up of the MAN, *now little more than a skeleton, lying by the gateway.*

NARRATOR *off* : And, growing childish in old age, he begs the very fleas to persuade the Guard to change his mind and allow him to enter.

12. The gateway (as in 10), light streaming from inside it.

NARRATOR *off* : His sight is dimmed. But in the darkness he perceives a radiance, streaming immortally from the door of the Law.

13. Medium close-up of the MAN *lying by the lighted gateway, hand raised.*

NARRATOR *off* : And now, before he dies, all his experience condenses into one question, a question he has never asked. He beckons to the Guard.

14. Close-up of the GUARD *leaning over the* MAN.

NARRATOR *off* : Says the Guard : ' You're insatiable. What is it now? '

15. Closer shot of the same.

NARRATOR *off* : Says the Man : ' Every man strives to attain the Law. How is it then that in all these years no one else has ever come here seeking admittance? ' His hearing has failed, so the Guard yells into his ear : ' No one else but you could ever have obtained admittance.'

16. Medium shot of the brilliantly lit gateway, the shadow of the GUARD *on the left.*

NARRATOR *off* : ' No one else could enter this door. This door . . . was intended only for you, and now . . . I am going to close it.'

17. Medium long shot of the lighted gateway, the door almost closed. Loud clang as it ' closes '.

[¹*The last picture in the projector shows the gate about to close. The light goes out . . . and then we see the* NARRATOR *himself coming slowly towards camera.*

NARRATOR : This is a story inside history. Opinions differ on this point, but the error lies in believing that the problem can be resolved merely through special knowledge or perspicacity — that it is a mystery to be solved . . . A true mystery is unfathomable and nothing is hidden inside it. There is nothing to explain . . . It has been said that the logic of this story is the logic of a dream. Do you feel lost in a labyrinth? Do not look for a way out. You will not be able to find it . . . There is no way out.]

18. Dissolve to long shot of the gateway almost closed.

NARRATOR : This tale is told during the story called ' The Trial '. It has been said that the logic of this story is the logic of a dream . . . of a nightmare.

With these words the succession of images by Alexeieff ends in a dissolve. Music.

19. We are inside K's *bedroom. Close-up from above, at first slightly out of focus, of* JOSEPH K *sleeping peacefully in his bed. Normally he has another two hours' sleep left. However, now we hear the noise of a key turning in a lock, off. K opens his eyes.*

20. Low angle medium shot, as from the bed, of a double door opening slightly.

21. High angle medium close-up of K waking and sitting up.

K : Miss Burstner?

Camera pans left with him as he sits up, to show the door in the background. The silhouette of a MAN, *seen from below, comes stiffly through the doorway. The* MAN *shuts the door behind him.*

INSPECTOR A : You were expecting Miss Burstner?

K *is now seen from behind, sitting on his bed. The* INSPECTOR, *facing us in the background, goes to the window. Camera pans slightly left.*

---

¹ The following section in square brackets is taken from Welles's own scenario and does not occur in the film itself. Following this we give the remaining words of the narrator as in the final version of the film.

K : Why, no . . . no. What a . . . what an idea. Of course not.

INSPECTOR A *opening the curtains* : You spoke her name just now.

K : When? *He realises the stupidity of his question. He is only half awake.*

INSPECTOR A : When I came in — you addressed me as Miss Burstner.

K *taken aback* : Well, that's . . . that's her room you know. Er . . . what . . . what . . . what were you doing in there? *The* INSPECTOR *does not reply.* Who are you? What are you doing in here?

INSPECTOR A *impassively* : Miss Burstner frequently comes through that door during the night?

> *He comes towards the bed, seen from below. Above him can be seen the low ceiling of a modern apartment.*

K : Frequently? No, no, never, never. *A pause. Still with his back to camera, he nods towards the double door.* That . . . that door is kept permanently locked. Mrs. Grubach keeps the key. Just . . . just ask her. *He gets up, clad in his pyjamas, and goes to another door on the right, camera panning slightly with him.* Where is she? Does she know about you? *Opening the door which leads into the corridor and calling.* Mrs. Grubach! *Camera tracks in on the two of them.*

INSPECTOR A *turning to* K : You were expecting Mrs. Grubach?

> K *turns round, shuts the door nervously, then stands in the middle of his room.*

K : No . . . no. I'm . . . not expecting anybody, least of all you, whoever the hell you are.

> *As he speaks,* K *goes towards the double doors opposite his bed. Camera pans slightly left.*

INSPECTOR A : Where are you going?

> K *stops and turns to face the* INSPECTOR.

K *rubbing his hands together nervously* : Well, I think that Mrs. Grubach would like to know that there are strange people roaming around in her apartment in the middle of the night.

INSPECTOR A *back to camera, pointing to the double door* : You were starting in that direction, and that's Miss Burstner's room, isn't that what you told me?

K : Yes, it is, and I would very much like to know what's going on in there.

> K *has moved over to the double door. However, he stops at the*

INSPECTOR's *next words, and does not open it.*
INSPECTOR A : She isn't there now.

Camera tracks out in front of K *as he comes back towards the middle of the room. He passes in front of the* INSPECTOR *and goes and sits down on his bed. As he speaks he puts on his socks.*

K : Well, that's . . . not so very surprising. She . . . she gets in late sometimes. Very late, very late indeed. You are the police?

INSPECTOR A : She gets in very late?

K : Look, don't . . . don't go jumping to conclusions.

INSPECTOR A : What conclusions?

K : Well, the . . . the hours they keep in her night club are no fault of Miss Burstner's. Look, she'll be home any minute now, and . . . and I'm sure she'll be able to answer your questions for herself. *A pause*. You are the police?

K gets up and goes over to a chest of drawers. Camera pans and tracks left with him. He takes off the bottom half of his pyjamas, puts them in a drawer and puts on a pair of trousers, talking as he does so to the INSPECTOR, *who has followed him. (Still on page 3)*

INSPECTOR A : What makes you think we want to ask questions of her?

K : Well, I have . . . I have no opinion of it one way or another. It's . . . it's nothing to do with me. I . . . I scarcely know Miss Burstner. Of course, we are . . . we are fellow lodgers, but that's obvious. Is . . . she in some kind of trouble?

INSPECTOR A : What kind of trouble? Do you imagine we came here to see Miss Burstner?

K *laughing falsely* : Well, you certainly didn't come here to see me . . . did you?

A pause. K *looks at the* INSPECTOR *who does not react. He seems discouraged by the* INSPECTOR's *inhuman attitude and tone of voice.*

K *doing up his trousers* : Well, listen. You don't deny anything or affirm anything. You just stand there and stare at me in the middle of my private bedroom at . . . K *looks at an alarm clock standing on the chest of drawers* . . . 6.14 in the morning. I don't see why I should put up with it. You haven't even identified yourself or shown me your papers. *He has now taken a shirt out of the wardrobe.*

INSPECTOR A : Isn't that for you to do?
> *Annoyed, K goes over to another chest of drawers on the right. Camera pans and tracks to follow him. He takes out his identity papers and hands them to the* INSPECTOR, *who is close behind him, almost in the middle of the room.*

K : Oh, no! My papers — excuse me — my papers are in perfect order. Here, see for yourself.
> *The* INSPECTOR *puts the papers in his pocket without looking at them, while K watches him, trembling slightly.*

INSPECTOR A : Why don't you finish getting dressed?
> *As he replies, K takes off his pyjama coat, then puts on his shirt, walking as he does so towards the door on the right which leads out into the corridor.*

K : For your information, I am a man of regular habits, and getting dressed at 6.15 in the morning doesn't happen to be one of them. Still, I don't suppose there is any hope of getting any more sleep.
He opens the door and bends down.

INSPECTOR A : Where are you going?
> *Having picked up his shoes from outside the door, K shuts it again.*

K *in a loud whisper* : I take a bath in the morning if you must know. Why?

INSPECTOR A : If you're reluctant to dress in front of me . . .

K *in a whisper, buttoning his shirt* : And I dress in the bathroom.

INSPECTOR A : Oh?

K : Yes.

INSPECTOR A : Why?

K : Well, it's warm in the bathroom and it's cold in the hall. Any more questions?
> ASSISTANT INSPECTOR 1, *a seedy-looking character in plain clothes, opens the door and comes in.*

ASSISTANT INSPECTOR 1 : Why would you wanna dress in the hall?

INSPECTOR A *going out of the room* : Stay in here.

ASSISTANT INSPECTOR 1 *insistently* : Why would you wanna get dressed out in the hall?
> *K pick up his shoes and goes to the other end of the room by the first chest of drawers. Camera pans left with him. In the background* ASSISTANT INSPECTOR 1 *approaches.*

K *exasperated, his back to the* ASSISTANT INSPECTOR : I don't, I don't . . . *A pause.* But if I did not get dressed in the bathroom after I've finished my bath, I'd be obliged to walk down the draughty hall in my silk dressing robe right after getting . . . after . . . out of a warm tub. I hope you'll understand. *He bends down and puts down his shoes.*

Assistant Inspector 1 : You said you wanted to get dressed in the hall.

> *Still with his back to the* Assistant Inspector, *K tucks his shirt into his trousers as he talks.*

K : No, no, no, no, no.

Assistant Inspector 1 : Didn't you?

K : No! *He bends down again.*

Assistant Inspector 1 : Okay. You have it your way, mister. What do you wanna get all dressed up for anyway? You're not going anywhere. You're under arrest.

K *standing up having just put on his shoes* : You're . . . making a formal charge?

Assistant Inspector 1 : Oh, I couldn't do that, mister.

K *turning towards him* : Just exactly what is it I'm charged with?

> *A shadow appears on the ceiling behind them.*

Assistant Inspector 1 : You'll have to take that up with the Inspector. That was the Inspector who just left.

> Assistant Inspector 2 *appears on the right and approaches them. He looks about as unappetising as his colleague, and is walking up and down, reading from a small notebook.*

Assistant Inspector 2 *reading* : Proceedings having been started against you, until called for interrogation you will retire to your room . . . *As he speaks,* Assistant Inspector 1 *goes off to the right.*

K *at the mention of the word ' room '* : I'm in my room.

Assistant Inspector 2 *pausing* : . . . after . . . huh?

K : I'm in my room.

Assistant Inspector 2 : I can't help that, mister.

> *Camera pans and tracks to the right, tilting up, as K walks to the centre of the room buttoning his cuffs.*

Assistant Inspector 1 : You've got a lot of real nice shirts here, mister.

> *Camera pans right as K rushes towards* Assistant Inspector 1, *who has just opened the chest of drawers by the door and is*

21

poking around inside.

K : You leave those shirts alone.

ASSISTANT INSPECTOR 2 *begins to speak off, then comes into frame in back view on the right. We see the three of them from a low angle, K facing camera by the open door.*

ASSISTANT INSPECTOR 2 : You know something? You'd do a whole lot better to give them things to us. After they're impounded officially and carted off to headquarters, you won't know what happens to them shirts.

ASSISTANT INSPECTOR 1 *tapping K on the shoulder* : There's every kind of crookedness and bribery in them public offices. You know what I mean?

ASSISTANT INSPECTOR 2 : Now, we're your friends . . .

K *grabs at the open drawer as* ASSISTANT INSPECTOR 2 *moves towards it.*

ASSISTANT INSPECTOR 1 : Sure we are. *A pause.* You ought to give us some of them shirts at least.

The two men remain standing near the chest of drawers, while K, adjusting his shirt cuffs, goes over to the window. Camera tracks and pans left to follow him, still from a low angle.

K *shrugging his shoulders* : Well, it could be a joke, I suppose. An elaborate practical joke by some of my friends in the office.

ASSISTANT INSPECTOR 2 *off* : They're in there.

K *turning to the two policemen in astonishment* : Who's in there? *Intrigued, K goes to the double door which opens into* MISS BURSTNER'S *room.* ASSISTANT INSPECTOR 2 *moves across in front of the camera, which tracks in towards K.*

22. Reverse shot of the doorway from the other side as K opens it. The two policemen stand on either side behind.

23. Reverse angle medium long shot of MISS BURSTNER'S *room. On the far side three men turn round. They have been looking at some photographs lying on an upended trunk by her bed.*

24. Resume on K, bewildered.

K : You're from my office.

25. Resume on the three men, who greet K with ceremonious bows.

26. Resume on K.

K : Who brought you here?

27. Resume on the three men. One of them points at one of

22

the policemen behind K.

28. Resume on K. *He turns to* ASSISTANT INSPECTOR 2 *behind him.*

K : The police? *To the* ASSISTANT INSPECTOR. These clerks from my office — what have they got to do with it?

ASSISTANT INSPECTOR 1 *moves forward between his colleague and* K *and off to the right.*

ASSISTANT INSPECTOR 1 *off* : Rabenstein ...

29. Resume on the three clerks, ASSISTANT INSPECTOR 1 *in the foreground on the left.*

ASSISTANT INSPECTOR 1 *continuing* : . . . Kublick and Kaminer. Right?

K *off* : Leave those photographs alone.

ASSISTANT INSPECTOR 1 *moves forward as the* CLERK *on the right speaks, holding out a framed photograph.*

CLERK : I'm Rabenstein.

ASSISTANT INSPECTOR 1 *taking the photograph* : What's this? A dame, with some canaries.

K *off* : That's her mother. She was in the profession.

Camera tracks in as ASSISTANT INSPECTOR 1 *comes forward, holding up the photograph in front of him.*

ASSISTANT INSPECTOR 1 : A hell of a profession!

As the ASSISTANT INSPECTOR *speaks,* K *rushes in.*

K : Leave her things alone!

He snatches the photograph from the ASSISTANT INSPECTOR. *Camera pans right and tracks in as he goes angrily up to the clerks and replaces the photograph on top of the trunk.*

K *to the clerks* : You especially. *A pause.* K *addresses* RABENSTEIN, *who looks away, embarrassed.* Rabenstein, what are you doing here?

ASSISTANT INSPECTOR 1 *off* : Inspector said he thought it'd be sort of more . . . K *turns and comes towards him.*

30. Reverse angle medium close-up of ASSISTANT INSPECTOR 2 *writing in his book. He looks up as* K *enters and walks past him.*

ASSISTANT INSPECTOR 1 *off* : . . . unabusive, if they went with you to the office.

K : Unobstrusive!

ASSISTANT INSPECTOR 2 : So nobody'd notice anything . . .

K *halting, his back to the* ASSISTANT INSPECTOR : Unobstrusive

is the word you're looking for. *Contemptuously*: Unabusive!
... How can I go to the office if I'm under arrest?

ASSISTANT INSPECTOR 1 *entering from the right*: That don't need
to keep you from working — not at this stage. *He goes to stand
behind his colleague on the left, who is still writing in his book.*

K *half turning round*: He said I had to stay in my room.

ASSISTANT INSPECTOR 1 : He was reading the wrong page.

> *The three men turn to face camera as the three clerks appear
> in back view in the foreground. K makes a show of looking
> relieved, and leans against the door, grinning nervously at his
> colleagues as he speaks. The two policemen look on with stony
> faces.*

K : Well, this obviously isn't anything of any importance. Quite
honestly, I can't remember a single offence that could be charged
against me. It's obviously a mistake — something very trivial.

> *31. Rapid close-up from below of the faces of the three clerks.
> RABENSTEIN, on the left, grins back at K, then his smile fades
> as he catches the eye of ASSISTANT INSPECTOR 1.*
>
> *32. Reverse angle shot. K turns to face the policeman as he
> continues.*

K : But the real question is, who accuses me? Well?

ASSISTANT INSPECTOR 1 : What do you mean?

K : What authority do you have for these proceedings?

ASSISTANT INSPECTOR 1 *interrupting him*: Don't you worry about
that mister. ASSISTANT INSPECTOR 2 *walks away into K's bedroom.*

> *33. Long shot of K's bedroom, the immobile figures of the
> three clerks in the doorway in the background. As ASSISTANT
> INSPECTOR 1 goes off, ASSISTANT INSPECTOR 2 goes towards
> the window, bends down, picks up a book and starts to leaf
> through it. Camera tilts down and up with him.*

K *coming forward from the doorway*: I'm sorry to disappoint you,
but I'm afraid you won't find any subversive literature or porno-
graphy.

> *Camera pans briefly right as K starts towards ASSISTANT
> INSPECTOR 1, who is rummaging in a record cabinet near the
> door into the passage.*

K : Don't touch those record albums.

ASSISTANT INSPECTOR 1 *pointing at a record player*: What's this
thing?

K *wearily* : That's my pornograph . . . my phonograph.

ASSISTANT INSPECTOR 2 *bending down on the left* : What's this?

K : What's what?

ASSISTANT INSPECTOR 2 : A circular line with four holes.

ASSISTANT INSPECTOR 1 *starting to write in a notebook* : Circular . . .

ASSISTANT INSPECTOR 2 : No, it's not really circular, it's more ovular.

K : Don't write that down, for heaven's sake!

ASSISTANT INSPECTOR 1 *simultaneously* : Ovular. *He continues to write.* Why not?

K *ironically* : Ovular!

ASSISTANT INSPECTOR 1 *glancing at* K : We can't not write it down just because you say we shouldn't.

K *wearily rubbing his forehead* : Ovular isn't even a word.

ASSISTANT INSPECTOR 2 *in back view in the foreground* : You deny that there's an ovular shape concealed under this rug?

ASSISTANT INSPECTOR 1 : He denies everything.

K : Mrs. Grubach's husband was a dentist. *A door opens off,* K *turns.* Oh, here she is now. Mrs. Grubach! Mrs. Grubach!

> *Camera pans right as* K *rushes to the door into the corridor, calling after her; then, receiving no answer, he comes back towards the centre of the room, camera panning left to follow him.*

K : This was Dr. Grubach's office.

ASSISTANT INSPECTOR 2 *moving across frame from left to right* : That don't matter. She can't come in here.

> *Camera pans left and tilts down with* K *as he bends down over the plate on the floor and explains how the dentist's chair was screwed to it.*

K : The dental chair was screwed to these four places in the floor. *In the background we see the legs of* ASSISTANT INSPECTOR 1 *as he closes the door on the three clerks.*

ASSISTANT INSPECTOR 1 : You want some good advice, mister?

K : What?

ASSISTANT INSPECTOR 1 *coming forward* : I wouldn't want the others to hear about it.

K *looking up at him* : Oh, now you want money I suppose? Well, you've got the wrong man!

Assistant Inspector 1 : That's what they all say.

K *getting up and going angrily towards the door* : I mean bribery! I don't happen to believe in it.

Assistant Inspector 1 : Bribery?

Camera pans right as he follows K to the door. K opens it.

Assistant Inspector 1 : Now wait a minute. Have I asked you . . .

34. Low angle medium close up of K coming out of the door.

Assistant Inspector 1 : . . . to give me anything . . . sir? Mister?

K *snatches a shirt from* Assistant Inspector 2 *who is standing in the passage.* Assistant Inspector 1 *follows him out and stands by his colleague.*

Assistant Inspector 2 : We're . . . we're leaving, mister.

Assistant Inspector 1 : You're not going to be one of them trouble makers now, are you?

As he speaks, the camera tracks sideways, panning from a low angle, to follow K as he goes into Mrs. Grubach's *kitchen. We see him from the side.* Mrs. Grubach *is busy at the stove.*

K : Mrs. Grubach.

Mrs. Grubach *turning round, embarrassed* : Good morning, Mr. K. I've got your breakfast ready. *As K goes towards a corner of the kitchen, carrying a shirt, she goes off to the right.*

Assistant Inspector 1 *to* Mrs. Grubach *off* : Listen, ma'am, I wish you'd tell him. He doesn't really think that he's guilty, and he should keep it to himself — see what I mean? At this stage of the game, this kind of thing makes a very lousy impression. Mrs. Grubach *comes back into the kitchen and looks at K for a moment as he stands with his face to the wall.*

K *turning round* : I'm afraid I owe you an apology, Mrs. Grubach.

Mrs. Grubach : Oh, no, Mr K.

K *passes in front of her as she picks up a loaded tray, and precedes her into the dining room. Camera tracks out in front of them. In the dining room,* Mrs. Grubach *puts the tray on the table. Camera pans left with her, cutting out K who reappears and sits down.*

K : This is not going to happen again, I can promise you that.

Mrs. Grubach : A lot of things happen in this world, Mr. K.

K : Yes.

Mrs. Grubach : You're my most valued lodger, Mr K. I think I owe it to you to be frank.

35. As Mrs. Grubach *finishes speaking, cut to medium close-up of the two of them,* K *in profile,* Mrs. Grubach *leaning forward.*

K : Yes, by all means.

Mrs. Grubach : It's your own good I'm thinking of. And I really have that at heart; perhaps more than I should. After all, I'm only your landlady. *A pause.* K *looks at her with a slight smile, which is both affectionate and condescending. She continues, leaning towards him.* Well, I've managed to have a few words alone with the Inspector . . .

36. High angle medium close-up of the two of them, Mrs. Grubach *in back view,* K *three-quarters facing camera.*

K *anxiously, looking up at her* : And?

Mrs. Grubach : It seems you are . . .

37. Reverse shot: K *is in profile, his landlady leaning towards him, facing camera.*

Mrs. Grubach : . . . under arrest, Mr. K.

K : Yes, I know that.

Mrs. Grubach *insistently* : But not the way a thief's put under arrest.

K *firmly* : No.

Mrs. Grubach : No . . . no with your arrest, I get the feeling of something abstract, if you see what I mean.

K *looking up at* Mrs. Grubach : I'd say it's so abstract I can't even consider that it applies to me. *He turns away again.*

Mrs. Grubach : Of course not, Mr. K.

38. Medium shot of the two of them. (Still on page 3)

Mrs. Grubach : Aren't you going to eat something?

K : Them two coming into my room the way they did . . . Well, I simply wasn't prepared. Now, in . . . in the office, for instance, I'm . . . I'm always prepared. You can't just crash in on me there. I should say not. People sometimes have to wait for weeks before they can get in to where they can speak to my secretary. *He pours himself some coffee.* No, my mistake was letting them start in on me before I even had a cup of coffee.

Mrs. Grubach : Coffee is always ready on the stove, Mr. K. I keep it there for Miss Burstner, when she gets in from work. Such ungodly hours she keeps!

39. A high shot of the two of them. K *starts to drink, then stops and looks at* MRS. GRUBACH.

K : Well, that's her profession.

MRS. GRUBACH : I suppose so.

K : The hours they keep in that night club . . .

40. Resume on K *in profile,* MRS. GRUBACH *facing him.*

K : . . . are no fault of Miss Burstner's.

MRS. GRUBACH : Perhaps not. *A pause.* You think I ought to offer those men some coffee?

K : What men?

MRS. GRUBACH *pointing* : The ones from your office. They're still in there.

K *leaping to his feet* : In Miss Burstner's bedroom? *Slight pan left. 41. Long shot of the dining room.* K *hurries towards camera, which tracks out in front of him as he comes through the door across the corridor and into* MISS BURSTNER'S *room, where he comes face to face with two of his fellow employees.*

K : My god! I thought you'd left. What are you doing here? Kublick? Kaminer?

They turn to face RABENSTEIN *off-screen. Camera tracks out in front of* K *as he comes out onto the balcony of* MISS BURSTNER'S *room, where* RABENSTEIN *is standing holding the framed photographs.*

K *angrily* : Rabenstein! Put those pictures back where you found them

[[1]K : I can't see any real reason for your presence. Who are you? Investigators? *They seem horrified by the suggestion.* But what are you looking for then? We hardly know each other. *He loses his temper.* And what's more, you're not even in my room, do you realise? KUBLICK *grimaces and shrugs his shoulders slightly, but does not reply, nor do the others.*

K *continuing* : Miss Burstner will be here any moment, and I wonder how you'll explain to her what you're doing in her bedroom.]

MRS. GRUBACH *enters in the background with a loaded tray as* RABENSTEIN *goes back into the room.*

MRS. GRUBACH : Here's some coffee for the gentlemen.

K *standing on the balcony, back to camera* : No, Mrs. Grubach!

---

[1] The following section occurs in the script but was not shot.

42. Reverse shot of K *on the balcony, facing camera.*

K : These people are not friends of mine! They came with the police and they should have left with the police.

43. Resume on Mrs. Grubach *and the clerks.* K *is in the foreground, back to camera.*

K : Please be good enough to show them to the door.

Mrs. Grubach : Yes, Mr. K. *To the men.* This way, gentlemen.

They go out, accompanied by Mrs. Grubach.

44. Resume on K, *facing camera. He watches them go, leaning against the door which opens onto the balcony. The facade of the apartment block opposite can be seen in the background. (Still on page 3)*

45. Reverse shot as K *begins to speak. The three clerks turn as they go out.*

K : What are you, anyway? Informers?

46. Resume on K, *facing camera.*

K : What do you have to inform about?

47. Reverse angle shot. As the clerks go out of the door in the background, camera tracks out and pans right to show the Inspector *standing on the balcony.*

K *turning round angrily as he sees him* : And you're still here!

48. Medium shot of K *facing camera. The* Inspector, *in right foreground, turns to look up at the apartment building opposite. Music.*

Inspector A : You're attracting attention, Mr. K.

49. Low angle long shot of the building opposite, following the Inspector's *gaze. Heads appear at the windows.*

50. Resume on K *and* Inspector A. *Camera tracks out as* K *walks to the right, past the* Inspector, *who remains gazing up at the building.*

K : Attracting attention? *A pause. He turns to* Inspector A. I'd appreciate the return of my identification papers, please.

Inspector A : Do you seriously think that we don't know who you are? *Camera tracks out again as the* Inspector *walks past* K *along the balcony.* Really, Mr. K, you're not doing your case any good, you know.

K : Exactly what is this case you've been talking about?

Inspector A *still walking* : I'm not talking about it.

K : Well why not? Why don't you talk about it? What am I

charged with?

INSPECTOR A *stopping and leaning on the balcony* : It's not for me to talk about your case.

K : Inspector . . .

INSPECTOR A : Yes? K *walks towards him.*

K *insistently* : What's the charge?

INSPECTOR A *evasive* : Mr. K, you aren't claiming innocence, are you?

K : Naturally.

> *He walks round behind* INSPECTOR A *and leans on the balcony beside him. As he does so, camera pans briefly right, sinking down and tilting up to show the two of them in low angle medium close-up.* INSPECTOR A *takes out a notebook, the one used by the two assistant inspectors previously.*

K : I'm also claiming invasion of privacy and rank abuse of basic civil rights.

INSPECTOR A *opening his book* : Hold on. Not quite so fast.

K : Oh, I don't pretend to know the legal terminology, but I can get a lawyer to help me out about that. It also happens that a very well-known advocate is a close personal friend of the family's.

INSPECTOR A *writing in his book* : You aren't threatening to register an official complaint, are you?

K : Yes, I am, I am. And I might also mention a rather clumsy attempt to work me for a bribe! K *walks back past the* INSPECTOR, *who does not move, but looks down into the street.*

INSPECTOR A : There she comes — your friend, Miss Burstner.

K : Yes. *He comes back past the* INSPECTOR *again and looks down.*

> *51. High angle shot from the balcony of a taxi stopping in front of the building. A woman gets out.*

K *off* : Well, she's not exactly my friend. Not that it's any business of yours. Are you going to stay here all morning?

> *52. Resume on the two men. Turning away from the* INSPECTOR, K *holds out his hand to him, fingers spread, and continues to look down into the street.*

K : What are we going to do now? Take finger prints?

INSPECTOR A *looking at his notebook* : We can do that at the station.

K *turning round* : The station?

INSPECTOR A *impassive* : Where else could you register an official complaint?

> *Behind them we see* Mrs. Grubach *approaching from the other end of the balcony.*

K *turning away again* : Well, we can forget about that.

Inspector A : It's on the record. *Reading.* You did use the word threatening.

K : No. That was yours. *The* Inspector *carefully rereads his notes.*

Inspector A : What's this? What's this ' pornograph '?

K : Oh, don't try to make anything out of that.

Inspector A *surprised and suspicious* : No?

K : Not unless you've got a dirty mind.

> Mrs. Grubach *is now behind them.*

Mrs. Grubach *embarrassed* : Excuse me. *She makes as if to go, but* K *beckons her back.*

K : No, no, no. You . . . you stay, Mrs. Grubach.

Inspector A : None of this is going to show up very well on the record, Mr. K. *Reading.* My men say you even tried to stop them from putting this down.

K *looking at the notebook over the* Inspector's *shoulder* : Well, I tried to stop one of them from making a fool of himself . . . Yes, yes. Ovular.

Inspector A : What's that?

K : Ovular !

Inspector A : There's no such word. *A pause.* Mrs. Grubach's husband was a dentist? Now what's that got to do with your case?

K : I never said that it did.

Inspector A : Then why mention such a thing?

K : Simply by way of explaining that ovular sh . . .

Inspector A *writing* : . . . Ovular . . . shape.

K *somewhat indignant* : You go on solemnly writing it all down !

Inspector A : There has to be a record, doesn't there? But this foolish babbling — it's not going to make much of an impression, I can tell you that, Mr. K. It won't look well at all.

> *He closes his notebook and walks away.* K *and* Mrs. Grubach *watch him go.*

K : I'm glad he's gone. I was afraid he might start in on Miss Burstner.

> *53. Resume on high angle shot of the street. The taxi drives off, and* Miss Burstner *comes across the road. Music.*

54. *Resume on low angle medium close-up of the two of them.*
K *looking down* : Oh, she's on her way up. *He starts towards the apartment, then stops at* MRS. GRUBACH's *next words.*
MRS. GRUBACH : Later than ever.
K : Well, let's hope she was safely away last night before these men got into her room. What time does she go to work?
MRS. GRUBACH : I believe she has to be dressed — or undressed — for that first performance at midnight.
K : They have a supper show?
MRS. GRUBACH : Well, I don't know what they call it.
K : A supper show.
MRS. GRUBACH : Er, I'm sure I wouldn't know.
K : Oh, that's what they call it.
MRS. GRUBACH : I've never been inside one of those places in my life. Indeed, you may wonder why I continue to rent my second best room to a woman of that sort.
K : What do you mean?
MRS. GRUBACH : Why, theatricals, Mr. K. This isn't really the place for them as I'm sure you'll agree. *He tries to go, but she holds him back and continues almost imploringly.* You see, I . . . I didn't know. She came with her mother — a perfectly respectable woman. Also she seemed . . . and . . . and when she died . . . well, I . . . I'm always too soft hearted for my own good . . .
> K *angrily pushes her aside and walks away, then turns round and leans on the balcony a few feet away from her.*
K : Mrs. Grubach.
MRS. GRUBACH : Yes?
K : What are you trying to say?
MRS. GRUBACH : Well, I . . .
K *wagging a finger at her* : I get the impression you're hinting at something concerning Miss Burstner.
MRS. GRUBACH : Well, since you ask, Mr. K, she not only performs in that place — it's drinking afterwards, with men.
K : What I asked, Mrs. Grubach, was whether or not you were casting aspersions on the moral character of one of your own lodgers.
> *With these words, K goes into his own room leaving* MRS. GRUBACH *on the balcony, looking after him in bewilderment.*
> 55. *Medium long shot of K walking across his room and*

picking up his waistcoat from the chest of drawers by the door.
MRS. GRUBACH *off*: Mr. K, you shouldn't put it . . .

56. Low angle medium shot of MRS. GRUBACH *from behind, looking in through the window of K's room from the balcony.*
MRS. GRUBACH *continuing*: . . . that way.
K: Goodnight, Mrs. Grubach. *Carrying his waistcoat, he comes to the window and starts to draw the curtains.*

57. As MRS. GRUBACH *begins again, resume on medium long shot inside the room with K drawing the curtains.*
MRS. GRUBACH *off*: I wouldn't dream of giving her notice without definite proof.

58. Resume on MRS. GRUBACH *from the outside as K finishes drawing the curtains. She moves to another window on the left.*
MRS. GRUBACH: You have to admit, Mr. K . . .

59. Resume on the inside of the room.
MRS. GRUBACH *off*: . . . that it's in the interest of all my guests to keep our house completely beyond reproach.

As MRS. GRUBACH *continues, camera tracks out and pans left as K comes towards the chest of drawers in the corner, putting on his waistcoat. He stands in front of it, doing up his collar.*
K: Beyond reproach! *Irritated, he goes back towards the second window, camera panning right to follow him. He stands in front of it, buttoning his waistcoat as he addresses* MRS. GRUBACH. Mrs. Grubach, if you're going to start throwing people out of this house, you'd better start . . . *He reaches for the blind.*

60. Close-up of MRS. GRUBACH *in back view, with K facing her.*
K: . . . with me! *He violently pulls down the blind. It fails to catch and flies up again, turning rapidly on itself, while he strides across to the door of his room.* Goodnight, Mrs. Grubach!

61. Close-up of MRS. GRUBACH *from inside the room, the blind still rattling against the window in the foreground.*
62. Reverse shot, MRS. GRUBACH *in back view in the foreground, K at the door of his room.*
MRS. GRUBACH: You didn't understand!
K *with his hand on the door handle*: Goodnight, Mrs. Grubach!

63. Resume on close-up of MRS. GRUBACH.
MRS. GRUBACH *looking downcast*: Goodnight, Mr. K.
K *off*: Goodnight!

64. Medium long shot of K *inside his room. He opens the door and goes out.*

65. Low angle medium close-up of K *from outside the door as he peers out into the corridor in the apartment.*

66. Reverse angle long shot of the corridor. At the end by the front door, we see MISS BURSTNER, *who has just come in. She turns on the light.* K *is in the foreground, back to camera.*

K : Miss Burstner?

MISS BURSTNER *coming forward and perching on the hall table* : Yes?

67. Reverse angle medium shot of the corridor, MISS BURSTNER *in the foreground and* K *standing in the open doorway of his room. (Still on page 3)*

MISS BURSTNER *as she takes off her shoes* : Hmmm?

K : Good evening. *He glances out of the window.* Or good morning, rather.

MISS BURSTNER *removing one of her shoes from its plastic overshoe* : If you're stuck for something to say, try ' happy birthday '.

K *buttoning his waistcoat* : Oh, it's your birthday? Is that why you're coming home so much later than usual?

MISS BURSTNER *moving towards him* : I didn't . . . I didn't know you kept track of . . .

68. Reverse angle medium close-up of the two of them, K *on the right,* MISS BURSTNER *coming forward, extracting her other shoe from its plastic overshoe as she continues.*

MISS BURSTNER : . . . my hours Mr. . . . *Looking very tired she passes in front of* K *and goes off to the left.*

K *calling after her* : Oh, I . . . didn't mean that. 'Course it's . . . it's none of my business . . .

69. Reverse angle long shot of the corridor, K *on the left,* MISS BURSTNER *approaching her room at the end.*

K : . . . what time you come home at night . . . it's nobody's business.

70. High angle medium close-up of MISS BURSTNER *standing by the door of her room. She looks at him for a moment.*

MISS BURSTNER *wearily* : That's right. Goodnight.

71. Reverse angle medium shot of K *at his door.*

K : Happy birthday!

72. Resume on MISS BURSTNER. *She looks at him.*

73. *Resume on* K, *who is silent.*
74. *Resume on* MISS BURSTNER. *She smiles briefly and opens her door.*
75. *Long shot of the corridor.* K *watches as* MISS BURSTNER *goes into her room at the far end. Jazz starts to play softly off, and continues throughout the following sequence. Camera tracks backwards as he comes towards the door of* MISS BURSTNER'S *room, then pans round to show him from behind as he knocks on the door and opens it. We get a quick glimpse of* MISS BURSTNER *undressing.*

K : Oh, oh . . . excuse me, excuse me . . . No, no ! . . . No, no ! . . .
He quickly shuts the door and almost runs back to his room, camera panning left to follow him.
76. *Low angle medium close-up of* K *as he enters his room and paces round it, nervously twisting his hands; camera pans with him. There is a knock. Camera pans as he rushes to the door and opens it.*

K : Yes?
77. *Reverse angle shot of* K *opening the door to find* MISS BURSTNER *standing outside, silhouetted in the foreground, back to camera.*

K *smiling at her* : Well that's what I ought to have done, naturally.
MISS BURSTNER : What? . . . What ought you to have done?
K : Well . . . I . . . after I knocked, I should have waited for you to invite me to come in, as you did. *A pause.* Come in.
78. *Low angle medium close-up of* MISS BURSTNER. *She stands in the doorway, in her dressing gown, and leans her head against the doorpost.*

MISS BURSTNER : You're not getting any funny ideas, are you?
K : Of course not.
79. *Reverse shot of the two of them. Camera pans left as* MISS BURSTNER *moves across and leans back against the other side of the doorway.*

MISS BURSTNER : Just because I knocked on your door.
K : No, but . . . that's what I mean. You did, didn't you, so . . . why don't you?
They look at each other. She smiles briefly.
MISS BURSTNER : You're a nice boy . . . but I'm not in the mood for it . . . It's been a long hard night.

K : Yes, hasn't it?

MISS BURSTNER : What do you know about it?

K : I was talking about myself.

MISS BURSTNER : That's what they all do. What else do they ever talk about? So give me a rest will you?

K : All right.

MISS BURSTNER *loudly* : All right what?

K : Well, I'll do whatever you say. But if you don't want me to talk to you and you won't come in . . .

MISS BURSTNER *shrugging and pointing across the corridor to* MRS. GRUBACH's *kitchen* : How can I come in? That old bag's just dying for a chance to throw me out.

K *glancing across the corridor* : Throw you out? Mrs. Grubach?

MISS BURSTNER : Out of the house. She's always got one ear open. *A pause. She sighs.*

K : What's wrong?

MISS BURSTNER : I told you . . . I'm tired.

K : I'm sorry.

> MISS BURSTNER *pulls herself together and moves off left.*
> *80. Long shot of the corridor. Camera tracks out in front of* MISS BURSTNER *as she comes towards her room, followed by* K.

MISS BURSTNER : I've forgotten what I wanted to ask you.

K : Maybe it'll come back to you.

MISS BURSTNER : Nothing ever comes back to me . . .

> *81. High angle medium close-up of* MISS BURSTNER *coming into her room and throwing herself on the bed.*

MISS BURSTNER : Big statement! Shut up everybody!

> *82. Long shot of the room.* K *appears round the door. He sees* MISS BURSTNER *stretched out on the bed, her dressing gown half open.*

K : I'm sorry. *He makes as if to go out, then comes back as she speaks.*

MISS BURSTNER *turning slightly towards him* : You're sorry, you're sorry, you're sorry — you always keep saying that. Who gives a damn?

K *standing by the open door* : I know . . . I'm sor . . . *He laughs.*

MISS BURSTNER : What's the big joke?

K : I almost said it again. *A pause.* You're right, of course, you're perfectly right.

Miss Burstner : Yeah?

K *shutting the door* : Nobody gives a damn. I know you don't.

Miss Burstner : I don't what? . . . Hey! Keep the door open!

K : I was agreeing with you.

Miss Burstner *half asleep* : Oh sure.

K opens the door again then comes round the end of the bed and sits down beside her. Camera tracks in, panning slightly left and tilting down towards them.

K : With what you just said.

Miss Burstner : I don't know what I've just said . . . Lousy national champagne. *She raises herself slightly, close beside him.* You know what they make it of?

K : No.

Miss Burstner : Neither does anybody else . . . No switching with the cold tea, either. Not tonight. The customer knew all about that one. He kept taking cute little sips out of my glass just to make sure I was getting myself putrefied!

Her dressing gown slips from her shoulder. She lies down again, her face close to his.

K : I'm sorry. *Camera tracks in on them.* Damn! There I go again!

Miss Burstner : Sssshhh!

K : It's never any use, is it — apologising? It's even worse when you haven't done anything wrong and you still feel guilty. I can remember my father looking at me — you know, straight in the eye. ' Come on boy,' he'd say, ' exactly what have you been up to? ' — and even when I hadn't been up to anything at all, I'd still feel guilty. You know that feeling? *She appears to be asleep. A pause. Then he continues.* And the teacher at school making the announcement that something was missing from her desk : ' All right, who's the guilty one? ' It was me of course. I'd feel just sick with guilt. And I didn't even know what was missing. Maybe . . . yeah, that must be it . . . unless your thoughts are innocent, one hundred percent . . . *She moves her head slightly. K leans towards her.* Can that be said of anybody? Even the saints have temptations. *He kisses her on the mouth. She puts her arm round his neck. (Still on page 3)* *Then he says* : What do you think?

Soft music.

Miss Burstner : I think you're crazy.

K : Maybe you're right. That would certainly explain . . . *A pause.*

No, I must reject that. I must reject everything but facts.

As they lie in each other's arms, she puts her hand in front of his mouth.

MISS BURSTNER : Sssshhh.

K *disengaging himself* : I am sane. I am innocent. I have committed no crime.

MISS BURSTNER : Three cheers for you. *She takes his head in her hands.*

K : You don't believe me.

MISS BURSTNER : Sure I believe you.

K : Well, be honest — what do you really think?

MISS BURSTNER : You've been out someplace.

K : Drinking you mean? Is that what you think? *He draws back.* That I've been out drinking and I'm drunk?

MISS BURSTNER *raising her head towards him* : Well next time you do, come to my place. I get a percentage on every bottle.

K : Miss Burstner, I have not left this apartment since I got back from the office last night . . . and I am not a solitary drinker.

MISS BURSTNER : Then what's your problem?

K : I'm under arrest.

MISS BURSTNER : Yeah? *She turns and sits up, staring at him.*

K : Unbelievable, isn't it?

MISS BURSTNER : How did it happen?

K : That's the point. I don't know how it happened. I haven't the remotest idea.

MISS BURSTNER : How do you know you're arrested? It isn't something you suddenly notice, like bleeding gums.

K : They woke me up and told me.

MISS BURSTNER : Are you sure you were awake?

K gets up and goes towards the door.

K : Yeah, well if you think I was dreaming, just look at those photographs.

He indicates the photographs lying face downwards on the top of the trunk. She sits in bed taking no notice and rearranges her night gown.

MISS BURSTNER : That's my mother.

K : Well?

MISS BURSTNER : In different poses. ' Burstner's Birds ' — a real good act. *A pause.* Let's leave my mother out of it. Do you mind?

42

K : Of course.

MISS BURSTNER : No offence.

K : No, no.

MISS BURSTNER : What did they get you for?

K : Oh, I wouldn't say they got me.

MISS BURSTNER : They arrested you, isn't that what you told me?

K : That's what they told me.

*He sits down in an armchair facing the bed. Camera pans
slightly left and tilts down, keeping both of them in frame.*

MISS BURSTNER : What's the charge?

K : That's what they didn't tell me. All I know is I'm supposed to
appear before some kind of interrogation commission . . . that's all
I know.

MISS BURSTNER *thoughtfully* : That's only for serious crimes.

K : That's what I thought.

MISS BURSTNER : Did they tell you that your crime wasn't serious?

K : No they didn't say that.

MISS BURSTNER : Maybe it's a gag or something.

K : That thought occurred to me at first . . . you know, some of the
fellows at the office . . . some kind of elaborate practical joke. But
. . . I didn't . . . I didn't really believe that. I just wanted to. Oh
it's awful how easy it is to get demoralised, isn't it? *A pause.* Oh,
of course, that's what they want. *A pause.* That's what they're
counting on. I'm not such a fool that I don't see that pretty clearly.

MISS BURSTNER *interrupting him* : You must have done something,
you must have done something!

K : Oh don't say that, don't you say that.

MISS BURSTNER : Or somebody's been telling lies about you.

K *waving his hands* : That could be it. Rumours . . . they're always
flying around for no reason.

MISS BURSTNER : Rumours?

K : Well . . . well at the office . . .

MISS BURSTNER : What kind of rumours?

K : You mean in my case? That's just it, I haven't the faintest idea.

*She gets up, looking alarmed. He does likewise. Camera tracks
in on them, tilting up.*

MISS BURSTNER : I hope to God it isn't politics!

K *simultaneously* : No, no, nothing like that.

She walks forward, pushing him backwards. He retreats in

43

surprise, camera panning with them. They stop, face to face.

MISS BURSTNER : Don't go dragging me into it!

K : Oh, Miss Burstner, I'm afraid we're just talking in circles.

MISS BURSTNER *furious* : That's not my fault! I'm not talking in circles. I don't even want to talk. What are you doing in here anyway?

K : Well, you invited me.

MISS BURSTNER : That's what you say.

K : Miss Burstner . . . please.

MISS BURSTNER : Please what? Listen if you're in trouble I'm sorry . . . I'm real sorry . . . but keep me out of it.

K : I did . . . I am . . . I told them you didn't have anything to do with me . . . but they wouldn't listen . . . it was maddening. *He points at the trunk.* And then when they started to mess around with your mother's photographs . . .

MISS BURSTNER : What! *She turns round to look at the photos and, noticing for the first time that they have been scattered, goes over to the trunk, camera panning right with her.* Who's been messing around with my mother's photographs?

> *She knocks one of them over. K reappears in frame as he comes towards her and props it up again.*

K : Oh, Rabenstein, I think it was. *Camera tracks out, panning left as he comes back towards the centre of the room.* But also the police.

MISS BURSTNER *coming towards him* : The police?!

K *turning towards her, back to camera* : Well that's what I've been telling you.

> *Furious, she pushes him backwards to the double door which connects with his room.*
>
> *83. Low angle close-up of K falling backwards through the double door.*

MISS BURSTNER *off* : Get out!

K : Miss Burstner!

> *84. Reverse angle medium close-up of MISS BURSTNER standing in the doorway, furious.*

MISS BURSTNER *shouting* : Get out!

> *85. Low angle reverse shot: K facing camera, MISS BURSTNER in back view in the foreground.*

MISS BURSTNER : Get out of here!

K : Miss Burstner, please ! *He glances anxiously towards the corridor.*
MISS BURSTNER : Get out and stay out and leave me alone.
K : Miss Burstner please . . . what will all the other lodgers think?
And Mrs. Grubi . . . Grubach? You'll wake her.
    86. Low angle close-up of MISS BURSTNER.
MISS BURSTNER *shouting angrily* : Get the hell out of my room.
    87. Low angle close-up of K *with an injured expression.*
K : I'm out.
    88. Medium shot of K *facing camera. In the foreground,* MISS
    BURSTNER *angrily closes the double door.*
    *89. Reverse angle medium close-up of the doors closing. A
    gong is heard. Fade out.*

    90. Fade in to medium close-up of K *carrying a parcel as he
    enters a vast open plan office. There are hundreds of secretaries
    seated at their desks, writing or typing. Noise of typewriters,
    over which the theme-tune by Albinoni plays loudly. The
    camera follows* K *from behind as he moves amongst the
    labyrinth of desks, then pans to the right and holds as he walks
    away.*
    91. A very high shot of K *as a* SECRETARY *comes down a stair-
    case in the foreground and calls him.*
SECRETARY : Mr. K !
    Camera pans to the right as K *walks towards a cloakroom near
    the bottom of the staircase.*
K : Good morning. If there's anybody waiting, I'll see them in a
minute.
SECRETARY : The deputy manager . . . he was looking for you,
Mr. K. I think he's in the hall. *A pause. They halt by the door of
the cloakroom.* And your cousin's here.
    At the SECRETARY's *last words,* K *turns round in great surprise,
    his hand on the door handle.*
K : My cousin? She's not supposed to come to the office.
SECRETARY : She said it was serious. K *goes into the cloakroom.*
    92. Low angle medium shot from inside the cloakroom as K
    comes in, turns on the light and puts his parcel up on a shelf.
    The DEPUTY MANAGER *appears at the door. (Still on page 4)*
DEPUTY MANAGER : K . . . K . . .
K *turning round, then indicating the parcel on the shelf* : Oh . . .

oh good morning sir. I was . . . was just arranging a little birthday surprise.

DEPUTY MANAGER *looking at him somewhat sceptically*: In here? In this broom closet?

K : Well . . . well I had this . . . this . . . this . . . this birthday cake for one of my fellow lodgers. I didn't think I ought to carry the thing into the office.

93. *Long shot of the two of them outside the office.*

K : Don't you agree?

Camera pans left then tracks out in front of the two men as they proceed side by side across the vast office. Noise of type-writers.

DEPUTY MANAGER : Who is she? K *laughs nervously.* If I'd only known about this lady before she could have been included in the invitation tonight. The theatre tickets are all booked.

K : Oh I know, I know.

DEPUTY MANAGER : There aren't any left.

K : Oh I know.

DEPUTY MANAGER : You'll understand I hope . . . Your girl . . . there won't be too much unpleasantness . . . *They go off to the right.*

94. *Medium shot of the two of them, in three-quarter back view. Camera follows them as they walk past a large window which separates the office from a reception area, through which can be seen the seated figure of a girl.*

K : Yes, well there's been some unpleasantness already so it can't be much worse. The cake is . . . actually my . . . my peace offering.

They stop face to face. The girl comes up to the window behind them.

DEPUTY MANAGER : If she doesn't take it in the right spirit K, she's not the girl for you.

The girl knocks on the window.

DEPUTY MANAGER *curious*: Who's that?

K *turns round in surprise, (Still on page 4) then faces the* DEPUTY MANAGER *again.*

K *embarrassed*: That's . . . that's my cousin Irmie . . . What's she doing here? *He looks back at the girl again.* What are you doing?

DEPUTY MANAGER *sceptical*: Your cousin, huh?

K *more and more embarrassed*: Yes, from the city . . . going to

46

school in the . . . the country . . . going to school in the city. I'm supposed to keep an eye on her.

DEPUTY MANAGER *half smiling* : We'll have to keep an eye on you, old man.

> *K laughs nervously: They both move to the window and K stands masking* IRMIE *from the* DEPUTY MANAGER.

DEPUTY MANAGER *seriously* : She looks pretty young.

K : Yes sir. *He turns and glares at* IRMIE, *who grins at him through the glass.*

DEPUTY MANAGER : There's a place for everything. Right K?

> *He walks a few feet away, camera panning with him and tracking in. He turns to face* K *who follows.* IRMIE *follows also on the other side of the glass. Other figures stand watching in the background.*

K : Oh she's never dared to come into the office before, sir, I can assure you of that.

DEPUTY MANAGER : You're a bright young man . . . one of our brightest. On the way up. *He pats him on the shoulder.* Don't spoil things for yourself.

K : No.

DEPUTY MANAGER : How old is she?

K : What? Oh Irmie? Um . . . she um . . .

DEPUTY MANAGER *seriously* : Can't be more than sixteen . . . if that.

K *grinning sheepishly, very embarrassed* : Yeah.

DEPUTY MANAGER *raising his eyes to heaven, and departing, his hands behind his back* : My God!

> *Camera pans briefly left as* K'S SECRETARY *reappears;* IRMIE *is still visible in the background, behind the window.*

SECRETARY *off at first* : Mr. K . . . the young lady . . .

K : Get her out of here. *He strides off left.*

SECRETARY : But she said that it's urgent.

> *95. On her last words, cut to low angle long shot of the office. Camera pans as* K *strides in and turns to his* SECRETARY *off-screen.*

K : I don't care what she says . . . just get her out of here.

> *Camera cranes up and tilts down to a high angle long shot of the office as* K *strides off down the aisle between the rows of desks. (Still on page 4) Music and noise of typewriters.*

96. A cock crows. Dissolve to exterior shot of K *arriving home from the office, carefully carrying the box with the cake in it.* MRS. GRUBACH'S *boarding house is part of a hideous complex of modern buildings standing on a piece of waste ground, which are oppressive and demoralising at the same time. It is dusk and a few lights are on in the apartment block.* K *walks away from camera and mounts an outside staircase. He stops as a woman passes, dragging a large trunk (which seems familiar) down the steps.*

K : I beg your pardon but isn't that Miss Burstner's trunk? *He comes back and tries to help the woman with it.*

MISS PITTL : And what if it is?

K : I thought I recognised it. *The trunk makes a clunking noise as it is dragged down the steps.* Here, you take the birthday cake.

MISS PITTL : I've got quite enough on my hands with this trunk.

K : Well yes, that's what I mean . . . well, let me help you with it. Here, take this.

MISS PITTL : No thank you.

K : Please . . .

MISS PITTL *emphatically* : No thank you.

K : Well a . . . at least let me call you a cab.

MISS PITTL : Not everyone can afford taxi-cabs, Mr. K.

K : Oh, you . . . you know my name?

They are now on the waste-ground. MISS PITTL *struggles along, dragging the trunk, followed by* K *with his parcel. (Still on page 4) The camera tracks slowly right with them. At this point we notice that* MISS PITTL'S *laborious progress is due not only to the weight of the trunk, but also to the fact that she has something wrong with her leg, which is in a brace. Each step she takes on the leg is accompanied by the noise of the brace.*[1]

K : Excuse me . . . you . . . you are a friend of hers, I gather. I wonder if you could tell me if she's home?

MISS PITTL : If by home you refer to Mrs. Grubach's apartment . . . *She stumbles and the trunk falls to the ground* . . . the answer to your question is no. *She starts off again laboriously.* Marika does

---

[1] The noise of the artificial leg is rendered on the soundtrack by the turning of a telephone dial.

have a home . . . but it's not at Mrs. Grubach's.

K : Marika?

Miss Pittl : Pardon?

K : I never knew her first name.

Miss Pittl *bitterly* : How ironic!

K : You say she has a home . . . you mean another home?

Miss Pittl : She has one now . . . luckily. *A pause. She continues to creak along.*

K : I wish you'd let me help you with that trunk. It seems quite heavy.

Miss Pittl : It is extremely heavy.

K : Well then.

Miss Pittl : I'll take it to her myself, thank you.

K : Take it to her? You'll take it to where?

Miss Pittl : I hope it's not your intention to follow me.

K : No, not at all.

Miss Pittl : Up to now you've been dogging my footsteps. *A dog barks.*

K : Well I hate to see a woman dragging a great heavy trunk like that . . . that's all.

Miss Pittl : Especially one with a physical disability, isn't that what you mean?

K : No, not at all, I . . .

Miss Pittl : Since you find the spectacle so unpleasant Mr. K, why not spare your feelings and remove yourself from the cause of your distress?

K : I'm sorry.

> *They stop for a second and then the procession continues for a moment in silence.*

K : Listen, the last thing I want is to annoy you, but . . . but I . . . I would like very much to know if . . . if Mi . . . Miss Burstner is moving or is planning to move and if so where to.

Miss Pittl : Anything else?

K : Yes . . . well yes . . . I'd like to know why . . . why she's moving.

Miss Pittl : And you have the unmitigated gall to pretend you don't know?

> *A pause. They have now drawn level with another apartment block. Rows of street lamps can be seen in the background. Camera pans slightly left as it continues to track along.*

K : Well no, how could I? I . . . I . . . I . . . I've just . . . just got home. I mean we did talk this morning but she didn't seem to be planning to move.

MISS PITTL : She wasn't Mr. K. It came as a very nasty surprise.

K : You make it sound as if I were responsible.

The trunk turns over. He helps her to right it and they walk on.

MISS PITTL : Do you pretend you have nothing to do with it?

K : I don't pretend anything. All I did was talk . . . Oh I did kiss her . . . I hope you're not . . . not trying to tell me that it's because I kissed her she's changing her address . . . just because I kissed her. I mean, after all she's a woman of the world. She . . . she works in a nightclub.

MISS PITTL, *who has been gasping with the effort of heaving the trunk along, now stops and turns to him.*

MISS PITTL : What are you insinuating?

K : Well nothing . . . but she'll have to admit she's a . . . she's a grown woman, not a minor. Somebody must have kissed her before.

He takes the trunk, relieving MISS PITTL *of the task of pushing it up a bank. (Still on page 4) A dog barks.*

MISS PITTL : Do you think this is a topic to be shouted through the public streets?

K : Oh hell . . . hell!

MISS PITTL : There's no need to curse.

K : Why am I always in the wrong without even knowing what for or what it's all about?

Camera stops tracking and pans slowly right to follow them up the slope.

MISS PITTL : That's not something I'm prepared to discuss with you Mr. K. *Sound of a train passing in the distance.* You'd better examine your own conscience.

K : Yeah, well there's nothing wrong with my conscience thank you, nothing at all.

He has got the trunk to the top of the bank. MISS PITTL *is climbing laboriously after him. He stops and leaves the trunk standing on its end, but hangs onto his parcel.*

MISS PITTL : Marika has been staying with Mrs. Grubach longer than you have Mr. K, don't forget that. She was very fond of that room. My poor little room is dark and damp and poorly heated. She won't be nearly as comfortable with me. *Sound of church bells.*

K : Well then why does she move for God's sake?

MISS PITTL : Please don't shout at me Mr. K. *She takes the trunk again and starts to go down the other side of the bank.* I'm a woman and a cripple but that doesn't mean I have to stand for your abuse. Go and scream at that Grubach woman.

The church bells continue to ring. K *calls after her.*

K : Wait a minute. You . . . you don't mean . . . *The church clock starts to strike seven.* Hell it's late. I'll never get dressed for the theatre. But first you gotta give me the truth. Now, did Mrs. Grubach ask her to leave?

MISS PITTL : I thought you didn't know what happened Mr. K.

97. Low angle medium close-up of K *standing on the bank of earth, watching* MISS PITTL *go, an apartment block and the lights of the town behind him.*

K *shouting after her* : Oh she did make a few uncalled-for remarks about Miss Burstner. I took exception to them . . . very strong exception. I told Mrs. Grubach in no uncertain terms that she was out of line!

98. High angle reverse shot of MISS PITTL *from behind, walking off into the distance with her trunk.*

MISS PITTL : Out of line indeed!

K *off* : You mean she . . .

99. Resume on K.

K : . . . just threw her out? *A lorry passes by in the distance.* Then I guess I . . . I guess I am responsible. Listen, Miss . . .

100. Resume on MISS PITTL, *seen from behind, dragging herself along.*

K *off* : Er . . . er . . . Mrs. . . .

101. Resume on K. *He looks at his parcel, ponders, then walks away from camera. Fade out.*

102. Loud music. Fade in to a low angle shot of a dimmed chandelier hanging from the ceiling of a theatre. The stage curtains part behind the camera, throwing light on the ceiling. (Still on page 37)

103. Longer low angle shot of the same scene. The shadows of the curtains move aside, revealing the tiered seats of the auditorium crammed with people. (Still on page 37) Applause.

104. Medium close-up of a row of the stalls. In the foreground, seen from below, K is applauding. On the left is a fat woman, asleep. (Still on page 37)

105. High angle medium close-up of K and several rows behind him. A paper which has been passed from hand to hand finally ends up with a YOUNG WOMAN *who is sitting just behind K. She taps him on the shoulder. Their conversation is almost drowned by loud music from the orchestra.*

YOUNG WOMAN : Excuse me, sir, excuse me.

K *turning round in surprise* : Yes ma'am?

YOUNG WOMAN *holding out the paper* : I've a note here for you.

K : Not for me.

YOUNG WOMAN : Yes it's for you.

K : Not for me.

YOUNG WOMAN *turning towards the audience behind her* : A lady passed this down.

K *looking round* : Where?

YOUNG WOMAN : It seems there's a man there waiting for you.

Unable to make out anyone in particular, K takes the note and starts to read it.

106. Medium close-up of K from below; his neighbour is still asleep. He reads the note, then gets up and leaves his seat, camera panning right with him.

107. High angle medium shot of K making his way between the rows of seats.

108. Low angle medium close-up of K's empty seat and his sleeping neighbour. Camera pans left as he passes a couple of rows back.

109. High angle medium close-up of K reaching the edge of the auditorium.

[¹*Shot of a stage curtain, brilliantly lit. Loud music. It is the overture to the* Merry Widow *which the orchestra is playing with typical Viennese panache. K is seated in the middle of the stalls with the* DEPUTY MANAGER, *wearing a dinner jacket. Light from the stage strikes him as the curtain rises. Someone taps him on the shoulder. He turns round and takes a piece of paper which is being held out to him. He reads it. On the*

---

1 Orson Welles modified this scene considerably during the shooting. His original plan was as follows.

*stage a line of pretty laughing girls against a brilliant décor à
la Maxim's. K is obviously furious at having to miss this first-
class show. But the note he has just received seems to offer
no choice.* He apologises to the DEPUTY MANAGER *and the
latter's wife; then to all the spectators he has to disturb in
getting out (the location should be an enormous opera house
in the style of the Palais Garnier, but should not be identifi-
able). The music echoes in the vast marble foyer. Here* K
finds the INSPECTOR *waiting for him.*

INSPECTOR A : You're looking very smart Mr. K. I'm very sorry
to spoil your evening.

K : Is that meant to be sarcastic?

INSPECTOR A : Not at all.

K : Am I supposed to wait quietly in my room, wearing a bath-
robe, waiting for the summons to arrive?

INSPECTOR A : You're the one who's being sarcastic, Mr. K. That's
not very helpful in a court of justice. I was sincerely sorry to have
to interrupt your evening.

K : You're taking me away?

Without answering, the INSPECTOR *moves away and* K
realises that he has no choice. He follows him.

INSPECTOR A : Obviously it was better for you to give up the time
devoted to your private life than that of your work.]

*110. In the next scene we are outside the auditorium of the
opera house which seems to be part of a complex of inter-
connected buildings, all in some way concerned with official-
dom: cultural affairs, town planning or local government.
They are monumental in aspect but dilapidated, sinister and
cold. They exude the melancholy atmosphere of all public
institutions.[1] In a low angle shot of the columned vestibule
we see* INSPECTOR A *standing stiffly beside a column. We hear
a door opening off.*

111. Low angle close-up of K *coming out of the door from
the auditorium.*

INSPECTOR A *off* : Mr. K.

112. Resume on the INSPECTOR.

113. Resume on close-up of K. *He sees the* INSPECTOR *and*

---

[1] This description is taken from Welles' original script.

walks forwards.

[[1]INSPECTOR A *leads* K *through a rehearsal room where an orchestra is rehearsing Albinoni's* Adagio.]

114. Resume on long shot of the vestibule. K *comes in from the right. (Still on page 37)* INSPECTOR A *walks past him to the left.*

INSPECTOR A : Come with me Mr. K.

The camera tracks forward, following the INSPECTOR *as he leads* K *out of the vestibule, along a corridor and through a door. In the following shots they at first appear to be behind the scenes in the theatre, changing gradually to the dingy corridors of administrative offices which at times look almost like cellars.*

115. Long shot of a murky corridor. The two men come through a door on the left and K *pauses to throw his note away in disgust, then follows the* INSPECTOR *as he walks off in the distance.*

INSPECTOR A : We're making every reasonable effort at this point to keep from interfering . . .

116. Low angle long shot of a similar scene. The two men pass by.

INSPECTOR A : . . . unnecessarily with the normal pattern of your life.

117. Low angle long shot of another dilapidated corridor, the two men coming towards camera. (Still on page 37)

INSPECTOR A : For instance, so you wouldn't have to request a special leave of absence from your office, we've arranged to fit in . . .

118. Reverse shot: camera tracks after them as the INSPECTOR *leads* K *into a dilapidated room.*

INSPECTOR A: . . . these interrogations outside your normal working hours.

They halt near a lamp hanging from the ceiling. Two plain-clothes policemen appear in the background. (Still on page 37)

INSPECTOR A : Step under the light Mr. K.

---

[1] Not shot. The *Adagio* by Albinoni is often used as a leitmotif in the film, e.g. during the credits, corridor scenes, tracking shots etc.

K *as he does so* : Who are they?

Camera tracks in as the INSPECTOR *walks towards the two policemen.*

INSPECTOR A *ignoring the question* : I can't expect you to know where the interrogation commission is sitting . . .

K : That's right, I don't.

119. Low angle close-up of the two policemen. Camera pans and tracks in on them slightly. (Still on page 37)

INSPECTOR A *off* : I've filled this out in your name.

120. High angle reverse shot: K facing camera in the background, the INSPECTOR *and the two policemen in back view in the foreground.*

INSPECTOR A *holding out a piece of paper* : And so you won't get lost I've drawn you a little map on the back.

K *taking the paper and walking away* : Thanks.

INSPECTOR A : You'll present that immediately on arrival.

K *turning round* : When is that?

INSPECTOR A : Immediately.

K : Tonight?

INSPECTOR A : I hope you won't have too much trouble locating it.

K *coming forward again and indicating the two policemen* : Well if I do, these two can always set me straight.

INSPECTOR A : What exactly do you mean?

K : Aren't they supposed to trail round after me wherever I go . . . observing my movements? *He turns and walks away again.*

INSPECTOR A : No . . . they aren't gonna follow you.

121. Low angle shot of the three policemen, all expressionless. INSPECTOR A *is in the foreground, the other two behind him. (Still on page 37)*

INSPECTOR A : That isn't their job.

122. Long shot of K walking away in the shadow of a wall.

123. Resume on the policemen.

124. Resume on K walking away.

125. Exterior shot. It is night. In low angle medium shot we see a statue completely covered in a sinister, loosely-hanging shroud. (Still on page 38) Camera tilts slowly downwards. Around the statue, at its feet, a number of people are sitting motionless, for the most part old and nearly naked. (Still on page 38)

126. Low angle long shot of several groups of people standing in silence. Behind them towers a vast, bleak building. They are clutching their clothes and a few personal possessions in their bare arms; large numbered cards hang from their necks. K *enters from the left and makes his way amongst them. (Still on page 38) Soft music.*

127. Low angle medium close-up of one of the groups. K *passes behind them. (Still on page 38)*

128. High angle long shot of the scene, K *in the centre of shot.*

129. Another similar shot. K *comes towards camera and goes off left. (Still on page 38)*

130. Low angle medium shot of K. *Camera tracks out in front of him as he walks between the groups and past the statue in the background.*

131. High angle medium close-up of a group of women. In the background K *enters the building.*

132. Very low angle shot of K *mounting a spiral metal staircase.*

133. Having arrived at the top of the staircase, K *makes his way through a labyrinth of dark corridors, camera tracking along beside him in low angle medium close-up. He finally arrives in a vast empty room; (Still on page 39) he looks around him and turns his head, hearing a noise of water, then walks towards a more brightly lit part of the room. The camera pans after him, revealing a young woman — HILDA — washing clothes with a tub and washboard in front of her. (Still on page 39) She nods towards the door.*

HILDA : Go right in there. *She watches him as he goes off left.*

134. Medium close-up of K *from behind as he opens a large double door. Inside is what appears to be a conference room filled with people. There is a gallery up under the roof also filled with people. General chatter.*

135. Long shot over the heads of the assembled company. They turn, and in the background a man rises to his feet behind a table on a crowded rostrum.

136. Medium shot of K, *standing by the door. He turns to go out again but comes up against* HILDA. *(Still on page 39)*

HILDA : I gotta close the door always after you. Nobody else must come in.

She shuts the door behind K; *then a small boy who is standing beside him takes* K *by the hand and leads him towards the rostrum. Camera pans with them.*
137. Medium shot of rows of men sitting at the side of the hall. Camera tracks left to a long shot of the rostrum.
138. As the EXAMINING MAGISTRATE *begins to speak, cut to a very high angle long shot of* K *from the gallery, being led across the packed hall by a small boy. The heads of two of the audience in the gallery are seen in back view in the foreground. Camera pans right to follow* K.

EXAMINING MAGISTRATE *who is in everyday clothes* : You should have been here one hour . . .
139. Long shot of K *from the side being led to the rostrum, camera tracking left with him.*

EXAMINING MAGISTRATE *continuing* : . . . and five minutes ago. These delays . . .
140. Medium shot of K *standing at the foot of the rostrum. (Still on page 39)*

EXAMINING MAGISTRATE *continuing* : . . . must not occur again. Please step up.

K *climbs onto the rostrum. He stands beside the magistrates and looks round nervously at the audience.*

EXAMINING MAGISTRATE : You are a house painter?

K *surprised* : No.
141. High angle long shot of the audience, who burst out laughing.
142. Long shot of the hall, K *standing on the rostrum in the background.*
143. High angle long shot of K *from the gallery as he begins to speak.*

K : The question from the examining magistrate about my being a house painter seems typical of this so-called ' trial ' that is being foisted upon me. *He takes the register from the magistrates' table and holds it up to show the audience.* Why the very notebook of the examining magistrate confirms what I say. These are the examining magistrate's records! *He throws it down on the table and it falls off into the front row of the audience. Laughter.* What's happening to me . . .

144. Long shot from the side of the hall with K *in the background. (Still on page 39)*

K : . . . is of no great importance. *As he continues to speak, a man picks up the register and passes it to another man near the rostrum.* But I think it is . . .

145. Low angle medium shot of K.

K : . . . representative of what's happening to a great many other people as well. *He comes round in front of the table.* It is for these others that I take my stand here . . . not for myself alone.

A MAN *shouting, off* : I support you in that.

146. As the MAN *finishes, cut to low angle long shot of the gallery, applauding loudly.*

147. Resume on K, *still addressing the audience.*

K : I have been arrested and perhaps, considering the magistrate's opening statement, perhaps they had orders to arrest some housebreaker, who may well be as innocent as I am.

148. High angle long shot of the audience applauding.

K : The arresting officers even tried to get me to bribe them . . .

149. Resume on K.

K : . . . to steal my clothes and shirts from me. I managed to keep calm. I asked them very simply why I was arrested. And what was the answer of your self-styled inspector? *He looks round at the judges.* If he were here he would have to back me up in this. Gentlemen, he answered in effect : ' Nothing at all.' He had arrested me. That was enough. *The* MAGISTRATE *makes a sign to the audience.* I notice that your examining magistrate has just given someone in the audience a sign. Well I don't know whether that sign . . .

150. A longer shot of the same scene.

K : . . . was meant to be a signal for applause or hissing, but I hereby publicly empower the examining magistrate to address his hired agents . . .

151. Resume on low angle medium shot of K.

K : . . . out loud. Let him say ' hiss now ' or whatever he wants.

152. High angle long shot of the audience turning to each other.

K : Can there be any doubt . . .

153. Reverse angle long shot of the hall, K *at the far end.*

K : . . . that behind my arrest, a vast organisation is at work?
154. Low angle medium shot of K from the side.
K : An establishment which contains a retinue of civil servants:
officers, police and others — perhaps even hangmen.
155. On K's final words, cut to high angle long shot of the audience rising abruptly to their feet. At the door in the background, HILDA is struggling in the arms of a MAN who is kissing her.
156. Long shot of the audience from the side, all looking towards the door, waving their arms and laughing.
157. High angle shot of the audience near the door, watching the struggling couple in the background and laughing.
158. Low angle medium shot of K watching from the rostrum.
159. High angle medium shot of the doorway. The MAN hoists HILDA onto his shoulder. (Still on page 39)
160. Very low angle long shot of the audience in the gallery rising to their feet.
161. Resume on K, looking alarmed. He jumps down from the rostrum and makes his way with difficulty across the room, camera tracking right with him.
162. Resume on high angle medium shot of the door. HILDA struggles as the MAN kicks it open.
163. Long shot of the hall. More of the audience rise to their feet, watching.
164. Resume on the door as the MAN exits with HILDA slung over his shoulder.
165. Very long shot of K standing in the middle of the room, bewildered by this unexpected and unusual sight.
K : I notice that every . . .
166. Low angle medium close-up of K indignantly addressing the audience around him. (Still on page 39)
K : . . . damn one of you here is an official of some kind. That means you've all come rushing in here to listen and nose out what you can about me. Half of you clapped; it was just to lead me on. *He moves off right.*
167. Medium shot of K pushing his way through the crowd. Camera tracks out in front of him, halting and panning right when he stops to address a particular group.
K : Get out of my way! Maybe you wanted some practice at fooling

59

an innocent man. Perhaps you found some amusement in the fact that I seriously expected you to be interested in justice.

168. High angle medium shot of K rushing out through the door.

EXAMINING MAGISTRATE *off*: One moment. K *stops and turns back.*

169. Reverse angle long shot of the EXAMINING MAGISTRATE *standing on the rostrum.*

EXAMINING MAGISTRATE: I merely wish to point out that to-night . . .

170. Resume on K standing in the doorway.

EXAMINING MAGISTRATE *continuing, off*: . . . you have thrown away with your own hands . . .

171. A closer low angle long shot of the MAGISTRATE.

EXAMINING MAGISTRATE: . . . all the advantages which an inter-rogation invariably confers on an accused man.

172. Resume on K. (Still on page 39)

K : Just you wait. *Sound of a gong.*

173. Low angle long shot from outside the doorway. K is seen from behind — a tiny figure, pulling the vast double doors shut with a crash. He backs away from them. Fade out.

174. High angle medium shot of K coming towards camera, past the window by the reception area in his office.

175. Low angle medium shot of K arriving at the top of the staircase leading down into the vast office. Camera tilts down, panning right and left to follow K as he comes down the staircase. In the background we see the rows of desks, all occupied. Noise of typewriters. K suddenly stops as he hears someone groaning off. He looks from side to side, then over the edge of the staircase, camera panning right with him, then upwards.

176. Reverse angle medium shot from below of the three clerks we saw earlier. They greet him with ceremonious bows.

177. Resume on K who returns their greeting with a nod.

178. Resume on the three men: they bow again.

179. Resume on K. Hearing more groans, he goes on down the staircase and approaches the cloakroom at the side, from which they appear to be coming. Camera pans right, following him from above. He pauses, then opens the door.

180. Medium close-up of what K *sees: the first* ASSISTANT INSPECTOR, *stripped to the waist and holding his shirt, but still wearing his hat, standing under the single lamp which hangs from the ceiling.*

ASSISTANT INSPECTOR 1 : Mister . . .

181. Reverse angle medium close-up of K, *astonished by the spectacle which he sees: on the right stands* ASSISTANT INSPECTOR 2, *fully dressed, on the left a stranger dressed in black leather. (Still on page 40)*

K *nervously* : What are you doing here?

182. Resume on ASSISTANT INSPECTOR 1 *under the lamp.*

ASSISTANT INSPECTOR 1 : We're going to be flogged.

183. Resume on K, *horrified. He looks down from* ASSISTANT INSPECTOR 1 *to his colleague on the right of frame.*

K : You're what?

ASSISTANT INSPECTOR 2 *leaning towards* K : We're going to be beaten.

184. Resume on ASSISTANT INSPECTOR 1.

ASSISTANT INSPECTOR 1 : It's all because of you, mister.

ASSISTANT INSPECTOR 2 *off* : Yeah!

185. High angle close-up of K.

K : Me?

186. Close-up of K *and* ASSISTANT INSPECTOR 2.

K : Why?

ASSISTANT INSPECTOR 2 : It's because you talked, mister. You complained about us to the authorities.

187. As ASSISTANT INSPECTOR 2 *finishes, resume on medium close-up of his colleague.*

ASSISTANT INSPECTOR 1 : You accused us of corruption.

188. Resume on K *and* ASSISTANT INSPECTOR 2.

ASSISTANT INSPECTOR 2 : You lodged a complaint.

K *looks round anxiously, shuts the door and leans back against it.*

K : I only men . . . I only mentioned it to the inspector.

ASSISTANT INSPECTOR 2 : And to the examining magistrate.

189. Low angle close-up of the MAN IN LEATHER, *who has hitherto remained silent.*

MAN IN LEATHER : Come on . . . let's get on with it.

190. Resume on K *and* ASSISTANT INSPECTOR 2. K *jumps nervously and looks round at the sound of the* MAN IN LEATHER's *voice, apparently noticing him for the first time. (Still on page 40)*

ASSISTANT INSPECTOR 2 : You accused us . . .

191. Rapid shot of the MAN IN LEATHER.

192. Resume on K *and* ASSISTANT INSPECTOR 2.

ASSISTANT INSPECTOR 2 : . . . of soliciting for bribes.

K : Well, you're not exactly innocent.

193. Resume on medium close-up of ASSISTANT INSPECTOR 1.

ASSISTANT INSPECTOR 1 *bitterly* : If you knew what kind of money we're expected to live on, you wouldn't be so hard on us.

194. Resume on K *and* ASSISTANT INSPECTOR 2.

ASSISTANT INSPECTOR 2 *speaking in* K's *ear* : I got a family to feed. Frank here wants to get married.

ASSISTANT INSPECTOR 1 *off* : Anyway, it's the custom for the . . .

195. Resume on ASSISTANT INSPECTOR 1.

ASSISTANT INSPECTOR 1 : . . . arresting officers to get the prisoner's body linen.

ASSISTANT INSPECTOR 2 *off* : Yeah!

196. K *and* ASSISTANT INSPECTOR 2 *again.*

ASSISTANT INSPECTOR 2 *more and more urgently* : Wha . . . what difference can a few shirts make to anybody when . . . once he's arrested?

197. Resume on ASSISTANT INSPECTOR 1.

ASSISTANT INSPECTOR 1 : Nothing!

198. Resume on the other two.

ASSISTANT INSPECTOR 2 : Nothing at all.

K : Well it wasn't anything personal . . . I was just defending a principle.

ASSISTANT INSPECTOR 1 *off* : Didn't I tell you?

199. Resume on him.

ASSISTANT INSPECTOR 1 : I told you the gentleman didn't want us . . .

The MAN IN LEATHER *strikes* ASSISTANT INSPECTOR 1 *violently; his moving hand catches the light which is left swinging. 200. Low angle close-up of* ASSISTANT INSPECTOR 1 *as he tries to protect himself with his shirt.*

ASSISTANT INSPECTOR 1 *hysterically* : . . . to be punished!

201. Low angle close-up of K *and* ASSISTANT INSPECTOR 2. *They flinch as the* MAN IN LEATHER *strikes again.*

202. Medium close-up of them, including the MAN IN LEATHER *as he lunges forward.*

203. Medium close-up of the MAN IN LEATHER *from the side,* K's *anguished face in the foreground. The* MAN IN LEATHER *hits out with a leather belt and catches the lampshade a resounding blow, setting it swinging again.*

204. Low angle close-up of ASSISTANT INSPECTOR 1's *face. Camera tilts down to show his bare stomach. Sound of another blow and a grunt of pain.*

205. Close-up of K *in profile, flinching,* ASSISTANT INSPECTOR 2 *facing camera behind him.*

206. Low angle close-up of the MAN IN LEATHER, *his face contorted, as he lunges forward. A crash as he hits the light again.*

207. Medium close-up of K *and* ASSISTANT INSPECTOR 2, *with the* MAN IN LEATHER *on the left, lit by the swinging lamp. A groan from* ASSISTANT INSPECTOR 1, *off.*

208. Resume on low angle close-up of the MAN IN LEATHER *as he strikes again. Crash!*

209. Reverse angle close-up of ASSISTANT INSPECTOR 1 *trying to protect himself with his shirt.*

210. Resume on the MAN IN LEATHER. *Crash!*

ASSISTANT INSPECTOR 2 *off* : Even if we had . . .

211. Back to ASSISTANT INSPECTOR 1. *He flings up a hand.*

ASSISTANT INSPECTOR 2 *off* : . . . taken your shirts . . .

212. Medium close-up of K *and* ASSISTANT INSPECTOR 2 *lit by the swinging lamp. On the left, the* MAN IN LEATHER *turns to listen.*

ASSISTANT INSPECTOR 2 : And even if the authorities had found out about it . . .

213. Close-up of K *in profile, and* ASSISTANT INSPECTOR 2 *facing camera.*

ASSISTANT INSPECTOR 2 : . . . nothing would have happened if you hadn't gone ahead and . . .

214. Low angle close-up of ASSISTANT INSPECTOR 1's *face, intermittently lit by the swinging lamp. He looks anxiously from his colleague to the* MAN IN LEATHER, *both off-screen.*

Assistant Inspector 2 *off* : . . . denounced us.

    215. Resume on him in low angle medium close-up, leaning angrily towards K.

Assistant Inspector 2 : It's just because of you that we're . . .
The arm of the Man in Leather *comes in from the left and strikes him a vicious blow with the belt. (Still on page 40)*
    216. Close-up of K *from the side, starting forward with a moan, his hand over his face.*
    217. Close-up of Assistant Inspector 1 *from below, still lit intermittently by the swinging lamp.*

Assistant Inspector 1 : What kind of justice do you call that? We've all got clean records — me especially. *A pause. He nods towards the* Man in Leather. Take him for instance. If anybody had ever lodged a complaint against him, do you think he'd be where he is now?

[[1]Man in Leather : That's enough of that. Quit talking. *He hits him.*

Assistant Inspector 2 : Ow! You can't imagine how much it hurts.

Man in Leather *to* Assistant Inspector 2 : Come on. You as well. Take your clothes off.

Assistant Inspector 2 : Oh it's awful. *Taking off his coat.* You gotta get all undressed.]

    218. As Assistant Inspector 1 *finishes speaking, cut to close-up of* K *from the side.* Assistant Inspector 2 *is beginning to undress behind him.*

K *to the* Man in Leather : Look.

Man in Leather *off* : What do you want?

K *taking out his wallet* : If . . . if you could see your way through to letting him off just this once, I'd certainly appreciate it.

    219. Low angle close-up of the Man in Leather *on the right of frame.* Assistant Inspector 1 *rises into view under the lamp behind him.*

Man in Leather : What are you trying to do?

K *off* : Nothing.

Man in Leather : You planning to lodge a complaint against me?
    220. Resume on K.

---

[1] The following section of dialogue did not occur in the version screened.

K : No. I haven't lodged any complaint. Why, if I wanted those men to be punished I . . . I . . . I could just leave right now and . . . and close the door and . . . and close my eyes and ears and forget about the whole thing. But . . . but I don't think they should be punished. They're not to blame. *He turns momentarily to* ASSISTANT INSPECTOR 2, *who is standing anxiously behind him.* It's people . . .

221. Low angle close-up of K *on right of frame, turned towards the* MAN IN LEATHER *behind him, who is facing camera.*

K : . . . above them that should be punished. The . . . the authorities. The . . . the whole organisation. Now if it were one of the high judges . . .

222. Close-up of K.

K : . . . you were flogging I wouldn't mind a bit. I'd even . . . I'd even pay extra to encourage the good work.

223. Low angle close-up of the MAN IN LEATHER *on the right of frame.* ASSISTANT INSPECTOR 1 *stands watching in the background.*

MAN IN LEATHER : I don't take bribes . . . not in any circumstances!

224. Close-up of K. ASSISTANT INSPECTOR 2, *now stripped to the waist, but still wearing his hat, clings to him in terror. Music.*

ASSISTANT INSPECTOR 2 : Please, please, please, please, please try to get me off! I mean, Frank here, he's older than I am. He can take it. He's been punished before but . . .

225. Low angle close-up of the MAN IN LEATHER'S *grim face.*
MAN IN LEATHER *interrupting* : I can't wait any longer!

The following sequence of very rapid shots is accompanied by the crashing of the metal lampshade as the MAN IN LEATHER *catches it with his belt each time he strikes a blow.*

226. Resume on K *and* ASSISTANT INSPECTOR 2. *They flinch.*

227. Resume on low angle close-up of the MAN IN LEATHER. *He lunges forward, his face contorted.*

228. Close-up of K *and* ASSISTANT INSPECTOR 2 *facing each other in profile. The* ASSISTANT INSPECTOR *cowers under the blow and yells out.* K *gasps.*

229. Low angle medium close-up of the MAN IN LEATHER *lunging forward past* K *who stands agonised on right of frame. Crash!*

65

230. *Close-up of the* MAN IN LEATHER *lunging again.* ASSISTANT INSPECTOR 1 *stands behind, lit by the crazily swinging lamp.*

ASSISTANT INSPECTOR 1 : He won't have much . . .

231. *Low angle close-up of him.*

ASSISTANT INSPECTOR 1 : . . . trouble. He knows that.

232. *Low angle close-up of the* MAN IN LEATHER *lunging forward, teeth bared. (Still on page 40)* ASSISTANT INSPECTOR 2 *moans, off.*

233. *Reverse shot. In the foreground, on the left, the* MAN IN LEATHER *lunges across at the naked torso of* ASSISTANT INSPECTOR 2. *Between them at the back* K *turns to go out.*

234. *Reverse shot. The swinging lamp lights first* ASSISTANT INSPECTOR 1, *watching from the back of the room, then the* MAN IN LEATHER, *lunging forward in close-up.*

235. *Very low angle close-up of* K, *flinching as the belt strikes* ASSISTANT INSPECTOR 2's *shoulder in the foreground. Camera tilts down with the* ASSISTANT INSPECTOR *as he sinks to the floor with a groan.*

236. *Close-up of the* MAN IN LEATHER *lunging forward again.*

237. *High angle medium close-up of* ASSISTANT INSPECTOR 2 *clinging to the door, trying to ward off the blows.*

ASSISTANT INSPECTOR 2 : Don't go! Oh please!

238. *Very rapid low angle close-up of the* MAN IN LEATHER *lunging forward.*

239. *High angle close-up of* K *standing in front of* ASSISTANT INSPECTOR 2 *by the door. The belt descends and catches him on the hand. He groans.*

ASSISTANT INSPECTOR 2 : Don't leave me!

240. *The* MAN IN LEATHER *lunging again.*

241. *Low angle close-up of* ASSISTANT INSPECTOR 2 *shouting as he is struck.*

242. *The* MAN IN LEATHER: *another blow. The swinging lamp momentarily reveals* ASSISTANT INSPECTOR 1.

243. *High angle medium close-up of* ASSISTANT INSPECTOR 2 *clinging to* K *by the door. Camera tilts up.*

244. *The* MAN IN LEATHER *strikes again.*

245. *Close-up of* K *by the door, struggling to get out.*

ASSISTANT INSPECTOR 2 *behind him* : Don't leave me! Don't!

246. *Medium close-up of* ASSISTANT INSPECTOR 1 *with his hand to his throat. Camera tilts crazily up to the left as the lamp swings to and fro.*

247. *High angle medium close-up of* K *by the door. He succeeds in getting it half open and struggles to free himself from* ASSISTANT INSPECTOR 2 *who is kneeling, hanging onto his waistcoat. The* MAN IN LEATHER *strikes again from the left. The lamp swings at the top of frame.*

248. *Low angle close-up of the* MAN IN LEATHER *striking again.*

249. *High angle close-up of* K *trying to get round the door.* ASSISTANT INSPECTOR 2 *hangs onto him from the inside. The belt lands on his shoulder. He grunts and groans.*

250. *High angle close-up of* K *from the outside, backing out of the door.*

ASSISTANT INSPECTOR 2 *off* : Oh! Oh! No!

251. *Medium shot of* K, *outside, trying to free himself from* ASSISTANT INSPECTOR 2. *All we can see of the latter are his arms, which are extended through the doorway, hanging onto* K.

ASSISTANT INSPECTOR 2 *grunting and groaning off* : Don't!

K *finally frees himself and the door slams shut. He straightens up and leans against the wall, whimpering in terror. Camera pans left and tilts up as he comes forward, his injured hand pressed to his mouth. Music. He turns nervously as his* SECRETARY *calls him, off.*

SECRETARY : Mr. K.

K *in a trembling voice* : What?

Camera pans further left as she appears from the direction of the office and comes towards him.

SECRETARY : Mr. K there's a man in your office. He says he's your uncle Max. K *starts towards her.*

252. *Long shot of the big office.* K *and his* SECRETARY *enter through a double door which she closes after them. Camera pans as they make their way through the maze of desks. Noise of typewriters.*

253. *Another long shot.* K *comes towards camera, his* SECRETARY *a few yards behind. Camera cranes up and tracks along with him from above as he walks past the rows of desks and up onto a platform where his own desk is. A man is*

seated beside it.

K : Uncle Max!

MAX *turning round* : Well my boy?

    The SECRETARY *passes in the background.*

K : What brings you into town?

    His uncle gets up. The SECRETARY *enters and sits at the next desk as they talk. We see the two men in high angle medium close-up. Behind them is the vast office, with the numerous employees sitting at their work.*

MAX *embarrassed* : Joseph, is it true?

K : Yes it's . . . yes it's true enough I'm afraid.

MAX : And you're under arrest?

K *trying to shut him up* : Please Uncle Max, I'm trying to write a letter.

MAX : Very well then. Just go ahead with your work, my boy.

    Annoyed, his uncle turns and walks a little way away, looking across the vast room. K *meanwhile sits down at his desk.* MAX *turns round again.*

MAX : Don't mind me.

    K *picks up a pencil and turns it nervously in his fingers.*

MAX *coming back towards his nephew and leaning over the desk* : It's not a criminal case is it? K *tries to say something.* Well?

K *nervously* : That's . . . that's what they tell me.

MAX *throwing up his hands* : And you just coolly sit here! *A pause. Then, having sat down beside* K, *he thumps the desk with his fist.* K *jumps.* MAX *continues.* If you won't think of yourself . . .

K : What?

MAX : If you won't think of yourself, think of the family . . . our good name!

    The SECRETARY *comes up and hands a file to* K, *who takes it and leafs through it.*

K : How did you . . . find out about it?

MAX : Irmie told me on the long distance telephone.

    K *gets up, then sits down again. Behind him, the* SECRETARY *gets up and stands by her desk.*

K : Irmie?

MAX : Yes, poor little Irmie . . . whom you wouldn't so much as receive here in your office.

K : I can't hold lengthy conversations with family relatives during

68

working hours.

His uncle picks up his hat from the desk and gets up.

MAX *annoyed* : I suppose that applies to me too.

K *gets up and makes his uncle sit down again.*

K : Oh, Uncle Max !

MAX *sitting down and taking out a handkerchief* : Now my only thought when I made this long exhausting trip was just to try to help you. But no . . . *He blows his nose.* K *is still standing* . . . you don't want to even see me.

K : Yes of course I do but you must realise . . . *He sits down again. Behind him the* SECRETARY *does likewise* . . . how difficult it is . . . during working hours.

> *There is a commotion in the vast office. All the employees get up simultaneously.*

MAX : Well it looks to me as though your working hours are over, Joseph.

K *getting up* : Come on. *He steps down from the platform, going out of frame. His uncle follows.*

MAX : After all Joseph . . .

> *254. High angle long shot from the platform as they make their way away from camera through the crowd of hurrying employees.*

MAX *off at first, then appearing at bottom of frame* : I'm the nearest thing to a parent and a father that you can lay claim to in the world. Don't forget that.

K *over his shoulder* : Oh I don't forget it Uncle Max, believe me.

> *255. Another long shot of the hurrying employees. Camera pans then tracks forward after* UNCLE MAX *as he hurries to catch up with* K. *The* SECRETARY *falls in behind them, against the general stream.*

MAX : We've got to get some competent legal advice, Joseph.

> *256. High angle medium shot from the staircase. Camera pans as* K *runs up a few steps, followed by* UNCLE MAX, *and peers anxiously down at the door of the cloakroom.*

MAX : Things like this don't happen right out of the blue . . . and in a criminal case !

K : Please, Uncle Max. People are listening.

MAX *looking up curiously* : What's that?

> *257. Low angle medium shot of* K *peering down from the*

staircase, UNCLE MAX *beside him.*

MAX : Up there? K *looks up.*

   258. Resume on high angle shot.

K : A computer.

MAX : Oh? *He goes up the stairs and off to the right.*

   K *continues to stare anxiously over the stair rail.*

   259. High angle shot of the top of the stairs. The three clerks walk off in the background as MAX *comes up, followed by* K. *Camera pans and tracks left as they approach the computer — a low row of panels with lights.*

MAX : One of those electronic gimmicks?

K : Yes.

MAX : That give you the answer to anything?

K : Yes.

MAX *walking up to the computer, which is making a chattering noise* : Well?

K : Well what?

MAX : You want to know about your case don't you? Ask the machine.

K : It wouldn't be allowed. *They both stop, face to face.*

MAX : These things can always be arranged can't they?

K : Who would I ask? Uncle Max, I . . . I don't even know what I'm charged with.

MAX : Well that's one question . . . the brain thing ought to be able to figure it out for you.

   They walk on past the apparatus, camera tracking left with them to reveal a MAN *standing in the background, back to camera.*

K : Well she'd need the data : economic, sociological, psychological. Still, she might be able to handle it. *They both stop, with the* MAN *behind them.* She screens and processes personality tests. But first an awful lot of material would have to be fed to her.

MAX : Her? It's a she?

K : That's the way the experts talk about it.

MAX : I see. Like for a car or a boat — kind of affectionate?

K : Well, respectfully . . . more than that.

MAX : Love, terror?

K : I don't know.

MAX : Well if she's a woman I'd be careful. *He bursts out laughing.*

Suddenly we hear groaning. K turns and listens.

K *to* MAX : Wait . . . wait . . . wait a minute. *He runs off left.*

260. High angle long shot of the empty office from the gallery where the computer is. K runs in from the right, along the gallery, camera panning left with him. He draws level with the three clerks, who are standing impassively as the groans continue off, and stops, looking somewhat embarrassed.

K *to the employees* : It's a . . . it must be a dog somewhere. It . . . it . . . it's that little dog in the courtyard, you know?

The three employees watch without a word as K goes off.

261. High angle medium shot of him going down the stairs from the gallery. (Still on page 40)

262. Medium shot of UNCLE MAX *staring after him in bewilderment.*

263. Close-up of K from behind as he flings open the cloakroom door to reveal the two assistant inspectors and the MAN IN LEATHER *standing under the lamp.* ASSISTANT INSPECTOR 1 *has a piece of sticking plaster over his mouth. His colleague turns to K, holding up another piece of plaster.*

ASSISTANT INSPECTOR 2 : He's putting adhesive tape over our mouths. Don't worry, with the tape on you won't hear him scream.

264. Close-up of ASSISTANT INSPECTOR 2. *He sticks the plaster over his mouth and mumbles indistinctly through it.*

ASSISTANT INSPECTOR 2 *mumbling* : There . . . see? . . . Like that you can't hear a thing.

265. Close-up of K. Overcome by the scene, he slams the door shut and leans back against it, reflects for a moment, then goes off left.

266. Long shot of the computer. UNCLE MAX *is talking to the* MAN *we saw standing beside it.*

267. High angle long shot of the top of the stairs. K's shadow looms on the wall as he comes up.

268. Resume on long shot of UNCLE MAX *and the* MAN. K *enters from the left and goes up to them.*

MAX *turning towards* K : This gentleman says he's in charge of the electronic brain, Joseph.

MAN : Well, not in charge . . .

MAX : One of the technical experts anyway. You talk about data and facts; well, crime is a fact, isn't it? Suppose I'd committed a

71

crime or rather suppose I hadn't . . .

K : Uncle Max, these men are extremely busy.

MAX : It seems they work in shifts on the computer.

MAN : Yes, our night people have more leisure. After eleven they could show you.

K : That's all right thank you. Come along Uncle Max.

> *269. Reverse angle long shot of the computer and the gallery. K takes his uncle by the arm and leads him towards camera, which tracks out in front of them as they pass two white coated employees going the other way.*

MAX : I agree with you Joseph. All these fancy electronics . . . they're all right in their place, but not for anything practical.

K *embarrassed* : Please Uncle Max.

MAX : You're not going to try to tell me you think you can diddle your way out of a criminal charge with an adding machine. *They go off left. Fade out.*

> *270. We are outside the ADVOCATE'S apartment. Fade in to close-up of a judas window. Knocking on the door, off. The judas opens, revealing a pair of woman's eyes. The judas closes.*
>
> *271. Medium close-up of UNCLE MAX knocking at the door.*

MAX : Open up in there! We're friends of the Advocate.

> *The door opens and MAX enters, followed by K.*
>
> *272. Low angle medium shot of the two men entering. The young woman who has opened the door is wearing a white overall and carrying a large candle. Sounds of a storm off, and flashes of lightning are seen through the windows.*

MAX *striding past the girl into the hall* : We've got to see him on very important business. I don't care how busy he is, we've got to see him now.

> K *pauses in the doorway as he sees the girl. They look at each other for a moment. Then she shuts the door and walks off, followed by K.*

MAX *to the girl* : K's the name. Announce us will you? *Coming towards K, past the girl.* She doesn't look like a maid to me — more like a nurse.

> *Camera tracks in after them as they follow her down the hall. Every piece of furniture is covered with lighted candles. The girl — whose name is LENI — turns towards them.*

72

Leni: The Advocate is ill.

She walks on again. Uncle Max *follows her with* K, *a few feet behind.*

Max: Ill? You say he's ill? His heart again I suppose. He never was too healthy.

273. Reverse low angle shot as they come out of the hall and proceed through the labyrinthine apartment. Camera pans round to frame them from behind as they walk through another candle-lit room. (Still on page 73)

Max: This may be a strange hour to be paying a professional call, but good old Hastler isn't going to hold that against me. We used to go to school together. You've heard me speak of him I know. He had quite a reputation in the past.

Max *goes out through a door at the end;* Leni *pauses and lets* K *go through first.*

274. Long shot of Max *opening a door and coming into a dim corridor which leads into the* Advocate's *bedroom.*

Advocate *off*: Leni.

Leni *off*: Yes?

Max *simultaneously*: Albert it's me — it's Max, Albert.

Camera tracks out as he comes forward, followed by Leni *and* K.

Advocate: Leni, I told you I'm too ill for visitors. Don't let these people in. Go away!

Camera pans round to frame Max *as he walks towards the* Advocate's *bed which stands on a platform to one side of the vast candle-lit room.*

Max: Albert! Don't you remember me?

Advocate *petulantly*: No.

Max: It's your old friend Max.

275. Reverse angle long shot of Leni *and* K *entering the room.*

Advocate: Leni.

Max *simultaneously*: Albert.

Camera pans left as Leni, *followed by* K, *approaches* Max, *by the platform at the foot of the* Advocate's *bed. Sound of thunder off.*

Max *continuing*: Hello Albert.

Leni *gives* Max *an indignant look, then goes to the head of the bed and arranges the bedclothes. (Still on page 73)*

81

MAX: Had another of your attacks? Don't worry, you always get over them. Are they looking after you properly? *To himself.* Terribly gloomy in here. No lights. *He turns and steps down from the platform; camera tracks out as* LENI *comes round the end of the bed.* Power failure of course, but ... *Loudly, as* LENI *goes off right* ... and what about this nurse of yours eh?

276. *Medium close-up of the* ADVOCATE: *his face on the pillow is almost hidden by the smoke from his cigar. (Still on page 73)*

ADVOCATE: Who? Leni? ... Huh!

277. *Low angle medium shot of* LENI *as she returns, carrying a steaming towel. As she passes behind* K, *she playfully butts him; then she goes up to the head of the bed, camera panning left with her.*

ADVOCATE: Leni's a good girl ... a very good girl indeed. Leni takes excellent care of me ...

278. *Low angle medium close-up of* LENI *and the* ADVOCATE.

ADVOCATE: ... Don't you darling?

She takes the cigar from his mouth and puts it in a glass on the bedside table. (Still on page 73)

MAX *off*: Miss! ...

LENI: Yes?

MAX *off*: Be kind enough to leave us alone for a while. I must speak to the Advocate on personal business.

LENI *covers the* ADVOCATE'S *face with a hot towel.*

ADVOCATE *to* LENI *in an undertone*: You can stay right here.

LENI *simultaneously*: He's ill. You can't talk business to him right now.

MAX *off*: Why you damn little ... minx!

As MAX *speaks,* LENI *leans over the* ADVOCATE *and, smiling, says something in his ear. He laughs under the towel and pats* LENI *on the buttocks. She tucks him in.*

ADVOCATE *from under his towel*: We can discuss anything in front of Leni. *She shushes him.* She's very, very discreet. LENI *goes off.*

279. *Slightly high angle medium shot of* MAX *with* K *in left foreground.* LENI *enters from the right and comes towards* K.

MAX: This doesn't concern myself.

ADVOCATE *off*: Oh?

MAX: It's not my own private affair.

280. *Medium close-up of the* ADVOCATE, *still under the towel.*

ADVOCATE : Whom does it concern?

281. Medium shot of MAX *seen slightly from below.*

MAX : My nephew. *Indicating* K *as he enters on the left.* I brought him here with me.

ADVOCATE *off* : Oh?

MAX : Joseph K.

282. Resume on the ADVOCATE.

ADVOCATE : Who? *He sits up and removes the towel from his face, staring off at* K. Joseph K?

283. Medium close-up of K. *Music.*

ADVOCATE *off* : I didn't notice you. So . . .

284. Resume on the ADVOCATE *getting out of bed; camera tilts up with him.*

ADVOCATE *smiling* : . . . So you came to see me about this case. That's good. It's a most . . . most interesting affair.

285. Resume on K. *Camera pans right as he approaches the bed, passing behind his uncle.*

MAX *quietly* : Careful now Joseph.

K *to the* ADVOCATE : Then you know . . .

286. A high angle shot of K *with the* ADVOCATE *standing over him on the platform by the bed.*

K : . . . about my case already.

ADVOCATE : How's that? I . . . don't understand.

K : I'm the one that doesn't understand.

ADVOCATE : It is your . . . case isn't it, that you want . . .

287. Low angle medium shot of the ADVOCATE *as he gets down from the platform and passes in front of* UNCLE MAX.

ADVOCATE *continuing* : . . . to consult me about?

MAX : Of course, it is. What's wrong with you?

K : Advocate Hastler seems to have heard about me and my case before we even thought of coming here.

The ADVOCATE *walks round the room, camera tracking and panning to follow him. There is a peal of thunder. He stops near* LENI.

ADVOCATE : Oh, in the circles I move in, all sorts of different cases naturally come up in discussion, and the more interesting ones stick in my mind — particularly something concerning the nephew of an old friend of mine.

288. High angle medium shot of UNCLE MAX. *As he speaks,*

camera pans right to show K *in the background.*

MAX : Of course — that's logical Joseph.

K *comes forward to address the* ADVOCATE.

K : You say you move in these circles — does that mean you're actually connected with the court?

289. A longer shot of K *and* UNCLE MAX, *taking in* LENI *and the* ADVOCATE *who are seen from behind, in foreground.*

ADVOCATE : With whom else should I associate if not with men of my own profession?

290. High angle medium shot of MAX *turned towards* K *who is standing back to camera in the foreground.*

MAX : That's certainly incontrovertible.

291. Low angle medium close-up of K. *He raises his eyes with a despairing expression.*

ADVOCATE *off* : I'm handicapped these days . . .

292. Low angle medium close-up of him with LENI *smiling behind his back.*

ADVOCATE : . . . by illness, but good friends from the law courts still visit me here from time to time, and I hear many interesting things from them. For instance, there's a dear friend of mine visiting me at this very moment . . .

293. Resume on K *as he turns his head, both interested and disturbed by what the* ADVOCATE *says.*

ADVOCATE : We were chatting here together . . .

294. Resume on the ADVOCATE *and* LENI.

ADVOCATE : . . . when you two burst in and took us by surprise. He preferred to withdraw with his chair and his table into the corner : the Chief Clerk of the law courts.

295. Resume on K.

K : Where?

296. A longer shot of K *from below,* LENI *and the* ADVOCATE *behind.* MAX *comes forward as* K *turns and looks away. Camera pans round the room, following his gaze. At the end of the room, a man is seated by a small table. The* ADVOCATE *appears, followed by* MAX.

ADVOCATE : I beg your pardon, sir.

297. Reverse shot of the ADVOCATE *from below. As he speaks, he comes forward into medium shot with* MAX *just behind him.* K *is seen in the background. (Still on page 73)*

ADVOCATE : I forgot to introduce you. This is my old friend K . . .
298. Long shot of the CHIEF CLERK seated.
ADVOCATE *off*: . . . and his nephew. I know, Sir, that you're
interested . . .
*299. A longer shot of the same scene including the ADVOCATE
and MAX, K in back view in the foreground.*
ADVOCATE : . . . in his case . . .
LENI *passes K, moving towards the ADVOCATE.*
*300. Close-up of K moving forward with an expression of
mingled curiosity and alarm.*
ADVOCATE *off*: Joseph K.
301. Long shot of the CHIEF CLERK. He gets up slowly.
ADVOCATE *in an undertone, off*: Leave us Leni.
*302. Long shot (as 299). LENI comes towards camera and goes
off, passing K, who turns and starts to follow her.*
ADVOCATE : Naturally, the Chief Clerk is a very busy man, but
since this case does concern us all, perhaps he'd stay for a moment
and advise us.
MAX : Oh my, yes . . .
Camera pans as the ADVOCATE goes off, followed by MAX.
*303. Long shot of the room. In the background, K watches
LENI as she comes towards camera.*
MAX *at the far end* : We'd certainly be honoured.
304. Close-up of K, watching LENI go. He moves forward.
CHIEF CLERK *off*: I can stay for only . . .
*305. Medium long shot of the CHIEF CLERK, coming towards
camera between the ADVOCATE and MAX.*
CHIEF CLERK : . . . a few minutes longer, unfortunately.
ADVOCATE : Oh yes, we know how pressed you are for time. *To
MAX. The* Chief Clerk will tell you, my dear old friend . . .
*306. Medium shot of K as he goes off to join LENI. Camera
tracks after him.*
ADVOCATE *continuing off*: . . . how I've defended a great number
of these cases . . .
*307. Reverse angle medium shot of K coming towards the end
of the room and peering after LENI.*
ADVOCATE *off*: . . . and even succeeded in winning a few of them.
308. Long shot of LENI walking off down the corridor.
CHIEF CLERK *off*: At least . . .

309. Low angle medium shot of the three men.

CHIEF CLERK : . . . partially.

ADVOCATE *somewhat put out* : Hah! Partially! *Hastily changing the subject.* The important thing now is to get our first plea ready. That often determines the whole course of subsequent proceedings.

CHIEF CLERK : However, in actual practice, the first plea is not usually read by the court at all.

ADVOCATE : Yeah.

MAX *simultaneously* : Oh? And why not?

ADVOCATE : Very often they simply . . . file it away.

> *The* ADVOCATE *stops at a noise of breaking glass which seems to come from the next room. They all look in that direction.*
> *310. Low angle medium close-up of* K, *who has been watching them. He turns also.*
> [[1]*No-one pays any attention to the noise, except* K, *who thinks that it must be in some way connected with* LENI.

K *feebly to the others* : Perhaps I'd better go and see what's happened.

> *He says this so quietly that none of the three men seem to have heard him. They are absorbed in their heated discussion. As discreetly as possible,* K *goes out towards the other room.*]
> *311. Resume on the three men, staring in silence.*
> *312. Resume on* K *in low angle medium close-up. He moves off left to follow* LENI.

CHIEF CLERK *at the far end* : I think that your friend here . . .

> *313. Low angle medium close-up of* K *as he leaves the bedroom and passes under a framed portrait on the wall. Camera pans and tracks with him as he walks across the next room.*

CHIEF CLERK *continuing off* : . . . should be warned that the case of Joseph K is likely to be followed through any number of courts . . . and sometimes a case . . .

> *The rest of his words are lost as music comes in over the sound of the thunderstorm. Camera pans and halts, framing* K *from behind, as he walks off in search of* LENI.
> *314. Camera tracks after* K *in medium close-up, three-quarter rear view, as he walks down a corridor, past a glass partition, and partly off to the left. We hear the three men continuing*

---

1 In the original script, Welles had the following.

their conversation off, without being able to catch what they are saying. LENI *is standing on the other side of the partition, a broken pane of glass in front of her. Camera halts to show* LENI *in front view,* K *reflected in the glass.*

LENI *to* K *who is facing her* : I broke the glass.

K : Why did you do that?

LENI : To attract your attention. I wanted you to come here to me. K *moves on.*

315. Low angle medium close-up of K *from* LENI'S *side of the partition, camera tracking right as he walks on.*

316. Resume on tracking shot from K'S *side,* LENI *seen through the glass,* K *reflected in it. He reaches the end of the partition and walks round it.*

317. Low angle medium close-up of them, face to face, LENI *back to camera.*

K : I was thinking of you, too.

LENI : In there you couldn't keep your eyes off me.

318. High angle reverse shot. LENI *looks up at* K.

LENI : And yet you left me to wait.

Camera pans with her as she goes and takes a coat from a hook on the right and comes back towards K. *She puts the coat around his shoulders.*

K : I . . . I . . . I couldn't just get up and walk out of the room, without any excuse. *He looks at the overcoat.* No . . . no, th . . . that's not mine . . . th . . . that's not . . .

LENI : You did it though.

They are now standing facing each other in profile.

K : Yes, I did. That's not my coat.

LENI : If you're going out, you'd better take this.

She holds him close to her by the lapels of the coat. (Still on page 74)

K : No, no.

LENI : You weren't wearing a coat. This is one of the Advocate's.

K : I'm not going out. I can't even stay here, I've got to get back to them.

LENI *moving her face very close to his* : I know you don't really like me, but I'm going to make love to you and then you won't be able to go.

K *embarrassed* : Yeah, but what will they say, back there?

Rummaging nervously in one of the pockets of the ADVOCATE'S *coat, he takes out a flask, frowns at it and puts it back immediately in the same pocket.*

LENI : You don't like me at all.

K : Well ' like ' is a . . . is a very feeble word.

LENI *letting go of him* : You've got a sweetheart?

K *shaking his head* : No.

LENI : I bet you do have one. A boy like you is bound to have somebody.

K *after a pause* : Well, as a matter of fact . . .

LENI *interrupting him* : Tell me about her.

K : Oh there's not much to tell really. I . . . I . . . I don't even know where she lives anymore. I've got her photograph.

LENI : Ah, you've got her photograph?

K : Uh huh.

He takes the photograph from his pocket and holds it out to her.

LENI *looking at it* : What is she? Some kind of an actress?

K : No, a dan . . . a dancer.

LENI *glancing up at* K : She's not so young, is she? I don't think I like her. She looks hard and selfish. A girl like that wouldn't be able to sacrifice herself for a man.

She slips the photograph back into K's *breast pocket; he takes it out again and puts it in an inside pocket.*

K : Not for me.

LENI leans forward and whispers in his ear.

LENI *whispering* : Has she got any physical defect?

K : What?

LENI : Has she got any physical defect?

K : Why . . . why no, of course not.

LENI : If you don't know where she's gone I guess she doesn't mean much to you or you'd find out.

K : I'll find out.

LENI *in a whisper, smiling up at him* : I've got a physical defect. I'll show you. Come.

Taking him by the hand, she leads him off towards another room.

319. They appear in medium shot at the door of a room which is as dimly lit as the rest of the apartment. LENI *shuts the door.*

Then camera pans as she goes and sits on some files and documents which cover more than half the room in an untidy heap. K follows her. She holds out her hand towards K.

LENI : Look.

320. Reverse angle close-up of LENI'S *hand. There are small webs of skin between the fingers. Behind it, we see K leaning forwards to look. (Still on page 74)*

LENI : The skin between my two middle fingers . . . *She laughs seductively.*

321. Low angle medium close-up of the two of them. (Still on page 74) Camera pans, following K, as he comes and sits close beside her. She follows him round, with her outstretched hand.

LENI : . . . It's like a web.

K *kissing her hand* : A web? What a pretty little paw.

LENI *puts her arm round* K's *neck and draws him to her.*

322. High angle medium close-up of the two of them lying amongst the files. They kiss. LENI, *lying on top of* K, *caresses him. (Still on page 74)*

LENI : You'd better go.

K : Go?

323. Close-up of their faces, LENI *leaning over K in profile. (Still on page 74)*

LENI : I'll . . . I'll say you weren't feeling well or something . . . That you needed some fresh air. *She starts to sit up.* I'll be back in a minute to let you out. I've got the keys.

K : The keys? Why? Can't I get out without any?

LENI : I don't want you locked out. The keys are to let you in yourself — during the nights, whenever you feel like it.

K *laughing* : Good.

324. High angle medium close-up of the two of them. K sits up and wraps the ADVOCATE'S *coat, which he is still wearing, around them both.*

LENI : I'll wait for you every night.

325. High angle long shot of the room. K and LENI *are seen from behind, under the coat, in each other's arms. Opposite them, facing the camera, is a large picture standing on the floor. (Still on page 75) Thunder and lightning, off.*

K : Who's that?

326. Close-up of K *and* LENI *under the coat looking at the picture.*

LENI : What? That picture?

K : Yes. That could be my judge I suppose.

327. Medium shot of the picture, standing on its side, intermittently lit by flashes of lightning.

LENI *off* : I know him.

328. Resume on the couple in high angle medium close-up. K *kisses* LENI *on the cheek as she speaks.*

LENI : He's not a big man like that. He's little — almost a dwarf. *She laughs.* But look the way he had himself painted. He's vain, of course, like everybody else here . . . I'm vain myself and it bothers me that you don't like me more than . . . *She kisses him as he speaks.*

K : You mean you've got high court judges coming here to see you?

LENI : Oh, no, he's just an examining magistrate.

K : Only an examining magistrate! What does a high court judge look like then? *They re-arrange themselves on the pile of files.*

LENI *laughing* : The throne and gown are just an invention. Actually he sits on a kitchen chair with an old horse rug doubled under him.

She laughs. Thunder. He kisses her.

329. A high shot of the room, the floor strewn with papers. Thunder and lightning.

330. Extreme close-up of LENI *and* K *kissing. She bites him on the chin. (Still on page 75)*

K : Ow!

331. Resume on high angle long shot. We see K's *arm waving among the rubbish.*

LENI : Do you always have to be brooding over your case?

332. Resume on the two of them in close-up.

K : Probably I don't think enough about it.

LENI *snuggling against him* : No, that's not the mistake you're making. You're too stubborn and too much of a trouble-maker, that's what I hear.

K *sitting up abruptly* : Who told you that?

LENI : You mustn't ask me for names. Just take my warning to rather try to be a little more co-operative.

K : Co-operative? Oh, brother! *He covers her with the coat again.*

333. A high shot. They are rolling in each other's arms.

334. Close-up of the two of them. K *is on top of* LENI, *the coat*

*hiding her face. He finally settles himself with her head in his
lap.*

335. Resume on high angle long shot. LENI *settles herself
against* K. *Thunder and flashes of lightning through the
window.*

336. Close-up of LENI *in profile, her head against* K's *thigh.*

337. High angle close-up of K.

338. Resume on LENI. *She rubs her cheek against his thigh.*

339. Resume on K *in close-up.*

ADVOCATE *calling off*: Leni! K *starts at the sound of the* ADVO-
CATE's *voice.*

MAX *off*: Joseph!

340. Close-up of LENI.

ADVOCATE *off*: Leni! *She starts also as the* ADVOCATE *calls her a
second time and* K *gets up behind her.*

*341. High angle medium close-up of the two of them. Camera
tilts up with them as they spring to their feet. Music.*

MAX *off*: Joseph!

*342. Low angle medium shot as they spring to their feet and
move away from camera.*

ADVOCATE: Leni, where are you? Leni darling . . .

*343. High angle long shot of the room as they scramble across
it.*

ADVOCATE *off*: . . . the clerk is leaving. *At these words* LENI *turns.*

344. Low angle medium shot (as 342). LENI *changes direction
and hurries back towards camera, coming down on the pile
of papers. (Still on page 75)*

ADVOCATE *off*: Come and see him . . .

345. High angle long shot (as 343).

ADVOCATE *off*: . . . to the door. *To the* CHIEF CLERK. Goodnight,
sir! . . . LENI *runs back and out through the door in the background,
while in the foreground* K *scrambles up the pile of papers to the
right.*

346. Low angle medium close-up of K, *who has climbed on a
pile of files and is looking down through a glass partition.*

CHIEF CLERK *off*: Goodnight.

MAX *off*: Goodnight.

347. Reverse angle long shot from above, K's *head in back
view in the foreground. Through the partition he sees the*

ADVOCATE *accompanied by* MAX *ushering the* CHIEF CLERK *out of the door. (Still on page 75)*

ADVOCATE : It's getting late.

MAX *simultaneously* : But Albert, what were you saying about advocates?

The ADVOCATE *retraces his steps, accompanied by* MAX.

ADVOCATE : Oh advocates! They do everything they can to discourage us. You should see the room they have for advocates in the law courts — it's so small.

MAX : Small? . . .

348. Resume on low angle medium close-up of K. *He drops down behind the partition.*

MAX : . . . the room for advocates?

ADVOCATE *simultaneously* : No ventilation . . .

349. High angle medium shot of K *scrambling across the files away from camera.*

ADVOCATE *off* : . . . just a tiny . . .

350. Reverse angle shot of K *scrambling down over the piles of paper, coming into medium close-up. Camera pans left and tilts down as he stumbles and falls.*

ADVOCATE *off* : . . . skylight up high. If you want to get a breath of air you have to have some other advocate . . .

351. Medium shot as K *arrives at the end of a corridor, then comes through a half-open door into another room, camera tracking out in front of him.*

ADVOCATE *off* : . . . to hoist you up on his back. For more than a year now there's been a hole in the floor.

MAX *off* : A hole, Albert?

K *takes off the coat and hangs it on the door, camera tracking in again and panning to follow him. At that moment we see the shadow of the* ADVOCATE, *and his cigar, as he approaches on the other side of the glass partition, accompanied by* MAX. *(Still on page 75)* K *hides in the shadows.*

ADVOCATE *off* : Not quite big enough to fall through, but if you stumble into it you find yourself with your leg hanging down into the corridor below — the very place where all your clients have to wait.

MAX *off at first* : I had no idea of the difficulties.

They have now arrived at the open door of the room where K *is standing silently, hidden in the shadows.*

92

Advocate : Yes it's all . . . *A pause. He turns and glances towards the room and at the door where the coat is hanging* . . . very humiliating ! *They move away.*

Max *off* : I only wish my nephew . . .

352. *Medium shot of* K, *who is hiding behind a pillar, watching them go.*

Max *off* : . . . could be hearing all this . . .

The rest of his words are drowned as music comes up over the noise of the storm. Confident that they are out of the way K *leaves his hiding place.*

353. *Long shot of the corridor.* K *appears coming towards camera, which pans with him as he goes through a doorway, pauses and goes off.*

354. *High angle medium close-up of* K. *Camera pans as he goes to a door and opens it. The* Advocate *and* Max *can be heard indistinctly between the claps of thunder, off.*

355. *Reverse shot. Camera tilts up to show* K *in medium close-up, standing in the doorway.*

356. *High angle shot of the room which is very small, like a cell, and almost entirely occupied by a bed. An old man in his shirt sleeves is sitting on a stool by the bed, looking up at* K, *who is partly visible just inside the door. Thunder and lightning. Music.* K *and the* Old Man *look at each other in silence, both seeming surprised and even horrified.*

357. *Low angle close-up of* K *standing inside the doorway.*

358. *Reverse shot of the* Old Man *sitting on his bed, looking depressed. Flashes of lightning illuminate the room through a circular window on the right.*

359. *Resume on* K.

360. *High angle close-up of the* Old Man *from the side.*

361. *Resume on* K. *He retreats towards the door.*

362. *Long shot of* Leni *entering the room full of files.* K *appears and waves his arm in the direction of the room he has just come out of.*

K : Who's that man ?

Leni : What man ?

K : That man in the there.

Leni : You shouldn't have opened that door. *They walk towards camera.*

K : Well, who is he?

LENI : Oh, him. He doesn't matter. Come here. *She lies down out of sight on the files.*

K *walking on* : What do you mean he doesn't matter?

LENI : Oh!

K *turning back and seeing where she is* : Oh no, no, no . . . I've got to go.

> *She gets up again and follows him across the room, camera tracking out in front of them.*

LENI : All right. *A pause.* These are the back stairs. You'd better pretend you've been waiting in the street.

> *They arrive at the glass partition.* K *comes out through a door in the partition which* LENI *closes behind him.*

LENI : Say you'd begun to feel faint — you needed some fresh air.

K : What's he doing in there?

> *363. High angle medium close-up of the two of them.* LENI *is behind the broken glass partition, looking up at* K, *who is in back view in the foreground. (Still on page 76)*

LENI : Waiting. He's a client. *She holds out a key.* Here's your key.

> *364. Reverse angle medium close-up.* K, *facing camera, finally takes the key from* LENI, *who is in back view in the foreground.*
>
> *365. Reverse shot (as 363).* LENI *looks up at* K.
>
> *366. Another reverse shot (as 364).*

ADVOCATE *off* : Leni.

> *367. At the sound of the* ADVOCATE'S *voice cut to reverse shot (as 365).* LENI *sighs and walks away across the room strewn with files. Camera tilts up slightly with her as* K *moves off right.*
>
> *368. Medium shot of* K *walking off down the corridor. He turns for a moment.*
>
> *369. Long shot of* LENI *going out of the room full of files and closing the door.*
>
> *370. Long shot of the dimly lit courtyard of the* ADVOCATE'S *house. It is dark and pouring with rain.* K *comes out from an archway at the back and crosses the courtyard, turning up his coat collar. (Still on page 76) Camera tilts up slightly as* UNCLE MAX *appears from the right.*

MAX *furious* : Joseph. Well?

K *pausing* : Well what? *He walks past* MAX *and off to the right.*

Max *turning and waving his arms* : You're facing a criminal charge. Do you want to make enemies? *He follows K off to the right.* Do you want to lose your case?

371. Dissolve to low angle long shot of K climbing a metal spiral staircase. Music.
372. Medium close-up of K at the top of the staircase. Camera pans and tracks forward following him down a corridor. He finally emerges into a large room. He seems to know where he is going and this time is determined to clear up his case. The room contains a bed, which he goes towards, then hears a slight noise and turns round. Camera tracks and pans, following him towards the source of the noise which is also the only source of light in the room. The pan ends on K watching Hilda in astonishment as she sits working at her sewing machine. Beside her is a standard lamp; the rest of the room is dark and bare.
(Still on page 77)

Hilda *without looking up* : Looking for somebody?

K *looking off left* : What's wrong? Isn't the court in session? *He moves off left.*

Hilda *getting up* : Not today.

373. High angle long shot of K entering the empty lecture room where he was interrogated previously.

K : Why isn't the court in session?

Hilda *off* : It'll be sitting tomorrow.

K : Are you sure?

Hilda *following K in through the big double door* : Sure. My husband's a guard here.

K *turning* : Guard? That man who was kissing you was . . .

Hilda *interrupting him* : That wasn't my husband who was kissing me, that was a law student.

As she speaks, K walks on into the room, spreading his arms in a gesture of resignation.

K : Uh huh?

Hilda : He's just a law student, but even so he's got influence.

K *turning towards her* : Influence huh?

Hilda : He's kind of important, he reckons.

K : He must be. You were making love right there . . .

374. A closer high angle shot of K advancing towards the

rostrum. HILDA *follows him. A table with some books on it stands on the rostrum in foreground.*

K : ... in the middle of the whole damn crowd.

HILDA : I guess we ruined that speech you were making, but what could I do with him? *As she continues K takes off his jacket.* Once he get's started it's ... *She runs forward as K reaches up, trying to get the books down from the table.* Hey! You can't touch those books — they belong to the examining magistrate!

K : I see.

    As HILDA *continues he climbs up onto the rostrum; camera pans and tilts up slightly with him.*

HILDA : It's not my fault. It's the rules. *A pause. She moves closer to him.* You do remember me, don't you, from last night? K *turns towards her and murmurs in assent.* My name's Hilda.

    K *is now standing on the platform beside the table, with* HILDA *standing on the floor below. (Still on page 77)*

K *looking at the books* : These are probably law books and of course I must remain ignorant of any law. *He picks up an elaborately bound book.* I must be condemned not only in ignorance ... *He breaks off.*

    375. Low angle medium close-up of K, *looking at the book with distaste.*

K : How dirty they are. *He blows the dust off and then goes and sits down beside the table and opens the book.* They really are dirty!

    376. Close-up of a page which carries a picture of a naked woman seen from behind, bending over.

    377. Resume on K, *seen from the opposite side,* HILDA *standing beneath him. He gets up, throwing the book down on the table.*

K : And these are the men that sit in judgement on me!

HILDA *seen from above, coming close to* K's *legs* : Listen, I'll help you. Wouldn't you like me to?

K : I don't see how you can if your husband's a courtroom guard here.

HILDA *caressing* K's *ankles* : I wanna help you, that's why I came in here.

    378. Low angle close-up of K.

    379. High angle close-up of HILDA *standing holding* K *by the ankles. (Still on page 77)*

HILDA : Even though ... it's forbidden.

K *off* : Well that's very nice of you but I wouldn't want you to get into any trouble.

380. Low angle medium close-up of K. *He sits down on the edge of the platform close to* HILDA, *who looks up at him.*

HILDA : No, you mustn't go away like that. Not yet. You've got the wrong ideas about me. Am I such a nothing in your eyes that you won't stay just a little longer when I ask you? *She leans forward, putting her hands on his knee. (Still on page 77)*

K : Well, I've . . . I've got plenty of time. I only came here thinking the court would be in session. You mustn't be offended when I ask you not to try to do anything about my case. The truth is I don't care at all how it comes out. And if they sentence me I just laugh at them. Oh, not that it'll ever come to that. Oh they might make a show of carrying it out in the hope of eventually getting money out of me, but they're wasting their time, I can tell you that. There's one thing you could do for me — tell that examining magistrate of yours that nothing on earth could ever induce me to give money to those precious . . .

381. High angle medium shot of K. *He jumps down from the rostrum in front of* HILDA.

K : . . . jurymen, nothing at all.

They remain facing for a moment. Then HILDA *picks up his jacket and leads him across the lecture room, past the wooden framework supporting the rostrum. Camera tracks in briefly and cranes down as they walk away.*

HILDA : Yeah, but you said the only ones who could do you any good were the higher-ups.

K *wearily* : I'm afraid so.

HILDA : Still, he's always writing books and they must go up to the real authorities. Last night, for instance, when the others had left he stayed on here . . .

382. Low angle shot from beneath the rostrum, showing its wooden supports, as the two of them walk along the end of the hall. They come towards camera which pans right with them.

HILDA : . . . real late . . . writing away. They even turned off the mains and I had to bring in a candle. Then my husband came home. We started to move furniture back in place and neighbours came in with some beer and we got to talking by candlelight and we just forgot about the examining magistrate altogether.

HILDA *stops, throws* K's *jacket onto the rostrum and sits down on a long seat against the wall.* K *stands in front of her for a moment, then comes and sits down beside her as she continues.*

HILDA : Then in the middle of the night I woke up and there he was, standing by our bed and shielding the candle with his hands to keep the light from hitting my husband. Not that he needed to bother — once my husband gets to sleep nothing wakes him. I was so startled I almost let out a yell, but the magistrate — he was real kind to me. He whispered that he had been in there all the time writing, and now he had come in to return the candle, and as long as he lived, he told me . . .

383. Medium close-up of the two of them, K *in three-quarter back view with* HILDA *facing him.*

HILDA : . . . he'd never forget the picture I made. That's what he said — the picture I made lying asleep in bed.

384. Reverse shot. K *looks nervously off,* HILDA *continues.*

HILDA : I just tell you this to show you . . .

385. Long shot of what K *is looking at. Seen through the wooden supports of the rostrum, a* MAN *is standing in the doorway at the opposite end of the hall, watching them.*

HILDA : . . . how busy he is writing out . . .

386. Resume on K, HILDA *in back view in the foreground. He looks nervously off and then back at her.*

HILDA : . . . these great long big reports.

387. Reverse shot, K *in three-quarter back view with* HILDA *facing him.*

HILDA : The one last night must have been about you, and somebody must read it.

388. Reverse shot (as 386).

HILDA : Besides, he's starting to take an interest in me.

K *looks nervously off again.*

389. Long shot of the MAN *in the doorway. He comes forward into the hall.*

HILDA : So maybe I could do you some good huh?

390. Resume on K *(as 388). He watches the* MAN *off-screen with increasing alarm as* HILDA *continues.*

HILDA : This morning he sent me a pair of stockings with the law student. Do you wanna see?

391. High angle medium shot of the two of them, the struts of the rostrum in the foreground.

HILDA : I got them on now.

She hitches up her skirt to show him her stockings (Still on page 77) and then pulls it down again as she too sees the man approaching.

HILDA : Look out! K *nervously looks at the* MAN *off-screen.*

392. *Long shot of the* MAN *approaching, seen between the struts of the rostrum.*

K *off* : Who's that?

HILDA *off* : It's Bert.

K : Bert?

HILDA : I know, he's ugly.

393. *Close-up of* K *and* HILDA *watching the* MAN.

HILDA : Did you get a look at those legs of his.

K *in an undertone* : Yeah.

HILDA : All the same I've got to go and be with him now.

K *turns anxiously towards her.*

394. *Medium close-up of the two of them,* HILDA *in three-quarter front view,* K *facing her in the foreground.*

HILDA *very softly* : I'll come back soon and then I'll go with you wherever you like and you can do with me whatever you want. *A pause.* What's wrong? Don't you believe me?

395. *Resume on* BERT *who has stopped for a moment. He comes on again, seen between the wooden struts of the rostrum. (Still on page 78)*

K : Why should I?

396. *Low angle close-up of the two of them.* HILDA, *in three-quarter back view, moves her lips close to* K'S *while he continues to look anxiously off at* BERT.

K : This could be a trap.

397. *Reverse angle close-up of the two of them.*

HILDA *whispering* : Are you afraid?

K : Who's this law student? A kind of henchman of the magistrate's?

HILDA : What of it?

K : I . . . I . . . I . . . I . . . I was thinking.

HILDA : Don't think. *She kisses him slowly. (Still on page 78)*

K : It'd kind of be a nice revenge to take you away from both of them.

HILDA : Why not?

K : Then some night after . . . the magistrate, after he's been staying up late filling out those long, long reports about me . . . he'd come to your bedside and it'd be empty. *He turns round, as does* HILDA.

> *398. High angle medium shot of the couple watching* BERT *approach, the wooden struts in the foreground.*
> *399. Medium shot of* BERT *clambering through the struts under the rostrum. Camera tracks out slightly and tilts up as he comes forward. (Still on page 78)*
> *400. Reverse shot with link on the motion as* BERT *emerges from under the rostrum. He is seen in close-up, back to camera, as* K *and* HILDA *rise to their feet in the background.*

BERT *aggressively* : Why don't you go?

> *401. Reverse angle medium shot of* BERT *standing just in front of the back of the rostrum, facing* HILDA *and* K *who are standing in left foreground.*

BERT *angrily* : You should have left the minute I came in!

K : You think so? HILDA *turns and looks at him.*

BERT *stepping forward* : That's what you're supposed to do. When I come in you get the hell out of here!

> *402. As* BERT *finishes, cut to reverse shot (as 400).* K *laughs. Camera pans right as he goes round behind* HILDA *and comes towards* BERT.

K : Well . . . I seem to detect the insolence of a future official of the court.

BERT *to* HILDA *as* K *finishes* : He shouldn't be allowed to . . .

> *403. Close-up of* BERT *looking grimly at* HILDA, *who is three-quarters back to camera in the foreground.*

BERT : . . . run around like this at large. That was a mistake.

> *404. Resume on high angle shot of the three of them (as 402).*

BERT : I told the magistrate.

K *to* HILDA : Come on.

BERT *loudly* : Don't try to be funny.

> *405. As* BERT *finishes, resume on close-up of him (as 403). He bends down and hoists* HILDA *across his shoulder.*

BERT : Come on.

> *406. As 404.* BERT *straightens up and carries* HILDA *off.*
> *407. Reverse angle medium shot of* K *standing by the back of*

the rostrum, watching them in amazement.

408. Close-up of K. Camera pans right as he picks up his jacket and starts after them.

K : Wait a minute!

A frantic chase ensues, seen in a series of fast tracking shots accompanied by fast, loud jazz.

409. Camera tracks behind K as he rushes down the corridor after the couple, pulling on his jacket as he goes.

HILDA *as they disappear round a corner* : It's no use!

410. Camera tracks beside K in low angle medium close-up as he hurries on, putting on his jacket.

K : What do you mean?

HILDA *off* : He sent for me. What can we do about it?

K : Who sent for you?

411. Medium shot, tracking rapidly sideways with HILDA, *slung backwards over* BERT'S *shoulder. They appear intermittently as they pass behind a series of screens covered in notices.*

HILDA : The examining magistrate.

412. Resume on K as he also passes behind the screens, camera tracking right to left.

K : The examining magistrate?

413. Track with HILDA *and* BERT *as they pass a gap in the screens.*

414. Another similar shot, taking in K, who is catching up with the other two.

HILDA : I don't want to, but this . . .

415. Camera tracks after HILDA *and* BERT *in high angle medium shot as they go down a corridor.*

HILDA : . . . ugly monster here won't let me go!

416. High angle medium shot of K. Camera pans briefly right as he follows down the corridor.

417. Low angle shot of the room where K met HILDA *previously.* HILDA *and* BERT *pass from left to right, camera panning with them. (Still on page 78)*

418. Similar low angle panning shot of K, who follows them across the room.

419. Resume on HILDA *and* BERT, *still moving fast. She calls back to K.*

HILDA : Sorry!

420. Resume on K. He pauses, looking after her.

421. Resume on HILDA *gesturing helplessly, camera panning left to right.*

HILDA : I got to.

422. Low angle panning shot of K as he follows them again.

423. Low angle forward tracking shot. K follows the couple out of the room and down a corridor.

424. Low angle reverse shot. Camera pans right as BERT *comes through a doorway carrying* HILDA, *followed by K.*

425. Reverse shot. HILDA *looks back as* BERT *carries her off down another corridor. (Still on page 78)*

426. Low angle reverse shot. Camera tracks in slightly as BERT *suddenly stops in front of a small door. The music fades, then continues more quietly. K runs up behind.*

K : Now listen!

He seizes BERT *by the shoulder.* BERT *bites his hand, making a noise like a barking dog, and he lets go.*

HILDA *to* K : Leave him alone. You want to ruin me? He's just obeying the orders of the examining magistrate.

K *retreating, discouraged* : All right. *To* BERT. Take her. *To* HILDA. You lied to me, didn't you? *He disappears through a doorway half way down the corridor.*

HILDA, *still slung across* BERT'S *shoulder, calls after* K : Why should I lie?

K reappears and comes back towards them. Camera tracks out.

K : You're not being taken to the examining magistrate.

HILDA *shouting* : Yes I am!

K *leaning against the wall* : You mean to tell me that the examining magistrate is waiting for you in a place like this.

As HILDA *replies, her voice becoming more and more strident,* BERT *finally gets the door open and the camera tracks out as he carries her inside.*

HILDA : Of course he is! These are the law court offices! Where else do you think he would be? *She closes the door behind them.*

Realising what HILDA *has just said, K rushes to the door and tries in vain to open it.*

K *in amazement* : The law court offices — in a place like . . . *He*

102

kicks the door furiously, then walks off down the corridor ... Hell!

427. Long shot of a gangway under a girdered roof with skylights in it. In the distance a MAN *approaches, bending low. Camera tilts up as he arrives in the foreground, straightens up and draws breath.*

GUARD : You're the defendant?

428. Reverse angle medium close-up of K, the GUARD *in back view in the foreground.*

K : My name is K.

429. Low angle medium close-up of K. Behind him is a mirror in which can be seen his own reflection, in back view, and that of the GUARD, *facing him.*

K : You're . . . the courtroom guard?

Camera tilts up to show the GUARD *himself, in three-quarter back view.*

GUARD : Yes, I'm her husband. It's Sunday night . . .

Camera pans slightly with him as he walks off to the left.

430. Link on the motion as the GUARD *comes into close-up from the right. He speaks bitterly, half to himself, in a heavy German accent.*

GUARD : I'm not supposed to work on Sunday night . . .

431. Resume on K in low angle medium close-up, his reflection behind him.

GUARD *continuing off* : But just to get me out of the way they send me out on these long . . .

432. Resume on the GUARD.

GUARD : . . . useless errands. *A pause.* That student — if my job didn't depend on it I would have squashed him flat against the wall long ago. *He glances downwards and continues with sadistic relish.* Right there, just a little bit above the floor. All splashed in blood with his arms and fingers and those bandy legs of his all twisted out and writhing like a smashed . . .

433. Medium shot of the GUARD.

GUARD : . . . cockroach! *He walks away from camera with his hands behind his back.* But now it's the examining magistrate.

K *appears on the right and camera tracks left with him as, walking several yards apart, they make their way through a lattice-work of steel girders.*

103

K : Isn't she to blame as well?

GUARD : She throws herself at him, and in my position there is nothing I can do about it, though if somebody would give him a good thrashing, just once . . . *He comes towards K. He's a coward you know. He'd never touch her again.*

Camera pans and tracks round till K is facing us. The GUARD passes in front of him.

GUARD : Only a man like you could do it. *He goes off left.*

K : A man like me. What do you mean?

Camera tracks left with K as he walks off after the GUARD.

GUARD *off* : They've arrested you, haven't they?

K : Yes.

GUARD *off* : Well then?

K : My being under arrest just gives me all that much more reason to be afraid of him.

As he finishes speaking, camera pans left as it tracks, taking in the GUARD again in the background.

GUARD : I heard about that speech of yours.

K : What about it?

Camera tracks in slightly as the GUARD comes towards him. They halt in medium close-up.

GUARD : I wouldn't have thought you'd be afraid at all.

K : I'm not. *He moves on.*

434. Medium close-up of K. He enters frame from the right and, as he continues to speak, he turns three-quarters back to camera to face the GUARD as the latter approaches.

K : I'm not afraid — not of him personally. I'm not afraid of any of them. But he does have influence, or so they say. He's certainly in thick enough with the examining magistrate, and God knows my case is prejudiced enough already.

GUARD *interrupting sternly* : It's a rule, none of our cases are prejudiced!

435. Reverse angle medium close-up of the two of them, the GUARD back to camera in the foreground.

K : I'm afraid I'll have to disagree with you about that. *A pause.* But it wouldn't necessarily stop me from taking care of that student.

436. Reverse shot (as 434).

GUARD : I'd be very grateful if you would. Come. *He steps forward.*

437. Reverse shot (as 435).

GUARD : Come. *He walks round behind* K, *who follows him through a door to the right.*

438. *Long shot of the* GUARD *leading* K *rapidly along the gangway towards camera.*[1]

439. *Low angle medium long shot of them passing along another gangway.*

440. *Low angle medium shot. They quickly descend a narrow metal staircase towards camera, under the girdered roof seen previously.*

441. *A longer shot of the same scene; camera pans right with them.*

442. *Low angle medium shot as they continue to descend the staircase.*

443. *Reverse shot of the same from above.*

444. *Low angle long shot of a hall with an arched ceiling. A line of men stand motionless on the left, piles of old papers on the right.* K *and the* GUARD *appear on a landing in the background, overlooking the hall.*

GUARD : These are the law court offices. *They move on down some steps.*

445. *Medium shot of a panelled door. The* GUARD *goes up to it, and camera tracks in as* K *appears from the left and follows him.*

GUARD *pointing*: That's where they are — my wife and the magistrate.

446. *Low angle close-up of the* GUARD, *searching almost desperately in his pocket for the key.*

GUARD *disappointed*: I don't have a key . . . for this one. *A pause.*

447. *Resume on the two men. The* GUARD *comes back past* K *and off to the right.* K *follows.*

448. *Medium shot of the two men from below. Camera tracks out in front of them as they pass along another gangway. A vast façade of lighted windows rises above them.*

K *looking down*: Who are these people? *They halt and the* GUARD *looks down also.*

GUARD : They are the accused. *(Still on page 79)*

---

[1] Their progress is accompanied by the leitmotif of the film, the *Adagio* by Albinoni.

449. Slightly low angle medium shot of the men seen previously, waiting in the arched hallway.

450. Resume on K and the GUARD (as 448). K goes off to the right as the GUARD continues to gaze down at the men.

451. Another low angle shot of the men, sitting or standing in dejected attitudes.

452. Low angle medium shot of K walking amongst the men, looking into their faces.

453. Medium shot of a group of seated men raising their heads to watch him. (Still on page 79)

454. Low angle medium close-up of K standing amongst more silent men. He looks at them uneasily and moves on.

455. Reverse angle medium long shot of K. He stops and looks around him.

456. Long shot of a solitary figure — an OLD MAN — seated on a bench at one end of the hall.

457. Medium shot of the seated men, watching.

458. Resume on long shot of the solitary figure. K, in back view, goes up to him and addresses him in a hectoring tone of voice.

K : You! Why're you here?

OLD MAN *getting up, facing* K : I'm waiting.

K : What is it you're waiting for? *The* OLD MAN *takes off his hat.*

459. Low angle medium shot of the GUARD as he stands watching from the gangway.

OLD MAN *off* : Yes, I handed in several affidavits . . .

460. Resume on the OLD MAN, in low angle medium close-up. He speaks in a tremulous voice. K stands three-quarters back to camera on the right. (Still on page 79)

OLD MAN : . . .That was some time ago. I'm waiting here . . .

461. Reverse angle medium close-up of K, the OLD MAN in back view in the foreground. Behind K several other men are gathering round to listen.

OLD MAN : . . . for the result.

K : You certainly seem to be taking a good deal of trouble over it.

462. Reverse shot (as 460).

OLD MAN : Why, yes. You see it's my case.

463. Reverse shot (as 461).

K : I'm under arrest. You don't see me putting up affidavits. What makes you think that kind of thing is necessary?

464. Close-up of the OLD MAN.

OLD MAN : I can't see exactly, but . . . I . . . handed in . . .

465. Resume on K *(as 463).*

OLD MAN : . . . my affidavits . . .

K : You don't believe I'm under arrest.

466. Close-up of the OLD MAN.

OLD MAN : Oh, yes, certainly.

467. Resume on K *(as 465).*

K : Why not? Why don't you believe I'm under arrest?

468. Close-up of the OLD MAN. *He says nothing.*

469. Low angle medium close-up of the GUARD, *still watching the scene from the gangway.*

470. Medium close-up of K, *looking bitterly at the* OLD MAN, *a crowd of onlookers behind him.*

K : What do you take me for?

471. Close-up of the OLD MAN, *smiling, at a loss.*

472. Resume on medium close-up of K.

K : You think I'm a judge?

473. Resume on the OLD MAN. *He says nothing.*

474. Resume on K. *He turns towards the men who have come up behind him, looks at them, then passes between them and walks away.*

475. Medium shot of the GUARD *from below, leaning down from the gangway. Music.*

GUARD *shouting* : You! Keep the passage clear!

476. Slightly low angle medium shot of the men below, who take off their hats and stand looking up at the GUARD.

477. Another similar shot, reverse angle, showing a vast arched window at the end of the hall.

478. Long shot of the hall, lit by antiquated lamps. K *comes forward into medium close-up and looks up at the* GUARD *off-screen.*

K : Can you tell me how to get out of here? I . . . I've had enough of this place.

479. Low angle reverse shot, K *in back view in the foreground, the* GUARD *on the gangway in the background.*

GUARD : You're going already? But you've hardly seen anything yet.

K *desperately* : I don't want to.

480. Resume on K in medium close-up (as 478).

K : I just want to get out of here.

GUARD : Well . . .

481. Medium close-up of the GUARD, still from below.

GUARD : You keep to the right along the passage . . .

482. Resume on K, who turns as the GUARD continues off.

GUARD : . . . and then you go . . .

483. Resume on the GUARD (as 481).

GUARD *waving his hand vaguely* : . . . to the second corner and then left along the lobby to the fourth . . .

484. Back to K, looking up at the GUARD.

K : You'd better show me yourself, there's so many passages . . .

485. Low angle reverse shot showing K, back to camera in the foreground, facing the GUARD who is leaning down from the gangway in the background, the vast lighted façade behind him.

K : . . . and lobbies, I'll never find the way.

GUARD : I've got a message to deliver and I've lost a whole lot of time because of you.

486. Resume on K in medium close-up.

K *shouting angrily and desperately* : Come with me !

487. Low angle medium close-up of the GUARD.

GUARD *leaning forward* : Not so loud. You want to bring all the officials down on us? Suppose they ask who you are — then you'll have to admit you're one of the accused.

488. Low angle shot of the two of them, similar to 485.

K : I'm not trying to hide anything.

489. Medium close-up of K against a long shot of the hall, the other men standing silently.

GUARD *off* : What'll I tell them?

K *with increasing despair* : The truth maybe. That I only came here because I wanted to see if the inside of this famous legal system was as loathsome as I guessed it was. And now I'm too depressed to want to see anything more. I just want to get out of here and be alone.

490. Low angle medium close-up of the GUARD watching him go. The music gets louder.

491. Medium shot of K as he stumbles into view from the

right, *behind a wire netting partition. A line of waiting men rise ceremoniously to their feet as he passes them and comes through a door in the partition. (Still on page 79) Camera pans left, then tracks out in front of K as he stumbles through another room, where another line of men rise to their feet. K pauses, looks nervously back at them, then goes off left.*

492. *Camera tracks and pans with K in medium close-up as he walks in from the right and bumps into the end of some shelves loaded with bundles of old papers. Finally he comes face to face with a* WOMAN *in glasses.*

WOMAN : What's wrong? You feel a little dizzy?

K : Yes.

Camera starts to track and pan with them as they move off, K bumping into the long rows of shelves loaded with dusty papers, the WOMAN *chatting cheerfully beside him.*

WOMAN : Oh, don't worry. Almost everybody has an attack like that on their first visit. It's the air. Then too all sorts of washing is hung up here to dry. You can't forbid the tenants to wash their own linen.

493. *Another similar tracking and panning shot. K hurries on faster past the silhouettes of waiting men in hats, pursued by the* WOMAN.

WOMAN : No, there's just nothing we can do about that I'm afraid.

494. *Medium close-up of K. Camera tracks out as he pushes his way past some more men and goes through a door to the right.*

WOMAN : Where are you going?

495. *Long shot down a long passage-way lined with shelves loaded with bundles of papers, and pigeon holes containing a card index system. The camera is tilted slightly upwards so that we can see a low ceiling of opaque glass through which comes a pale, watery light. K appears through a door on the left, knocking a few sheets of paper to the ground.*

496. *Another long shot of the corridor. A long line of men standing in front of the card index system rise slowly to their feet, taking off their hats.*

497. *Long shot of the corridor (as 495). The* WOMAN *appears and hurries up to K as he collapses slowly, clinging to the shelves. The* WOMAN *tries to hold him up.*

WOMAN: Do you want me to have you taken to the sick room?

498. Low angle long shot of the men watching. They start forward with grim faces.

K *off*: Please don't trouble yourself.

499. Reverse angle long shot of the corridor with the men in the foreground. Seen from behind, K staggers off, supported by the WOMAN, camera tracking along behind them.

K: If I could find a way just to get some air . . .

500. Low angle medium close-up of the two of them from behind, camera tracking after them.

WOMAN: It's not far now.

501. Reverse angle medium close-up of the two of them. Camera pans briefly right as K halts and leans against a corner of the shelving. (Still on page 79)

WOMAN: Here's the door right in front of you. K *looks completely demoralised.* Why don't you go out? That's what you wanted.

K *almost weeping*: Yes. Thank you. *He staggers off right.*

502. Medium shot of K. The WOMAN stands watching in the background as he staggers along past some more shelving and off to the right.

WOMAN: I'm not used to the fresh air.

[¹K, *horrified to find his legs giving way beneath him, trembles with the effort of keeping upright. A man — the* ARCHIVIST *— comes out of an office.*

ARCHIVIST: You know . . . *To the* WOMAN. I imagine this gentleman thinks that we'd do better to air all these offices.

He laughs unpleasantly. K *hears him and turns his head.*

K: That's it . . . If I could breathe . . . I'm not as bad as all that . . . I just need someone to support me under the arms a bit, so I can get to the door.

He spreads his arms so that he can more easily be supported. However, the ARCHIVIST *does not move. He stands with his hands in his pockets sneering at K.*

WOMAN *whispering to* K: Don't pay any attention to him sneering.

K, *who is totally downcast, does not seem to expect any explanation.*

WOMAN: This gentleman is the archivist of the enquiry service.

---

¹ The following scene in square brackets was cut in the editing.

110

People are so ignorant about our procedures that he has to answer their questions. You've noticed how smart he is . . . All the other employees are badly dressed . . . There's no point in spending money on clothes since we never leave the offices. We even sleep here . . . But we recognise that the archivist, who is in contact with the public, should look smart. We organised a collection to pay for his clothes . . . Unfortunately he destroys the whole effect by his sneer. It upsets people . . .

ARCHIVIST: I'm sorry to see that you're boring this gentleman with our little internal secrets. He's tired enough as it is. *He helps* K *to his feet.* Come on, old man . . .

K *agreeably surprised*: Thank you . . . Thank you very much . . . both of you.

WOMAN: Don't think the archivist has to help people who feel ill . . . He only does it out of the kindness of his heart.

ARCHIVIST: Sit down, old man, and get your breath back.

We see them once again in the large corridor, passing the OLD MAN *whom* K *spoke to earlier.* K'S *hair is dishevelled and hanging over his forehead. The* OLD MAN *appears not to notice him. He is only concerned to explain his presence. He stands humbly in front of the* ARCHIVIST *and does not really look at him.*

OLD MAN: I realise that a decision about my declarations under oath will not be forthcoming this evening. But I think I can just as well wait here . . . One never knows . . . I don't want to disturb anybody . . . I assure you . . .

ARCHIVIST: Why make these lame excuses? You board here, but so long as you don't disturb me you can follow the progress of your case from as near as you wish. You may sit down.

Gratefully, the OLD MAN *goes back to his place on the long bench.*

WOMAN *very quietly to* K: You see he knows how to speak to people . . .

ARCHIVIST: Don't you want to sit down?

K *shudders at the idea of joining the other defendants on their bench.*

K: Oh no, no thank you . . . I don't want to rest . . .

He staggers as if he were seasick and the corridor begins to move like a boat rolling in a rough sea. The walls swing terrifyingly to and fro. The WOMAN *and the* ARCHIVIST *seem to be trying to say something to him but all he can hear is the sound of waves coming from the end of the corridor.*

K : Louder . . .

His head rolls. He is ashamed, for he knows he is speaking quite loudly. Step by step he is carried along. Everyone is looking at him with their small piercing eyes. Suddenly a wall seems to open in front of him. He meets a current of fresh air.

WOMAN : Here's the door right in front of you . . . Why don't you go out? . . . Isn't that what you wanted?

K : Thank you . . . Thank you both . . . I'm going.

Outside he shakes them by the hand. He holds onto the WOMAN'S *hand as she staggers.*

WOMAN : You must let us go back in . . . We're not used to the fresh air.

The ARCHIVIST *sneers nastily. The door closes and* K *is alone. There is a long flight of steps which he must descend to get to the street. Can he make it? He tries, finds he can do it easily and suddenly starts running down the steps like a schoolboy.*]

503. Dissolve to low angle exterior shot of the courtyard of the court building. We see K *coming down the stone steps and past a statue. Camera tilts down.*

504. High angle long shot. He runs across the courtyard of the building between some columns.

505. Another long shot from ground level. K *crosses frame, dwarfed by huge columns.*

506. Medium shot of K *emerging between two columns. Music and bells off.* IRMIE *is hiding behind one of them, watching him. As he draws level with her she calls out.*

IRMIE : Hello!

K *stops and turns round. She comes towards him.*

K : Irmie! What are you doing here?

IRMIE : Well, I've been looking for you.

K : Why?

507. Low angle medium long shot of the two of them coming down the steps. IRMIE *trips down them like a child or a cripple, dragging her right leg.*

K : Uncle Max I suppose . . . checking up on me.

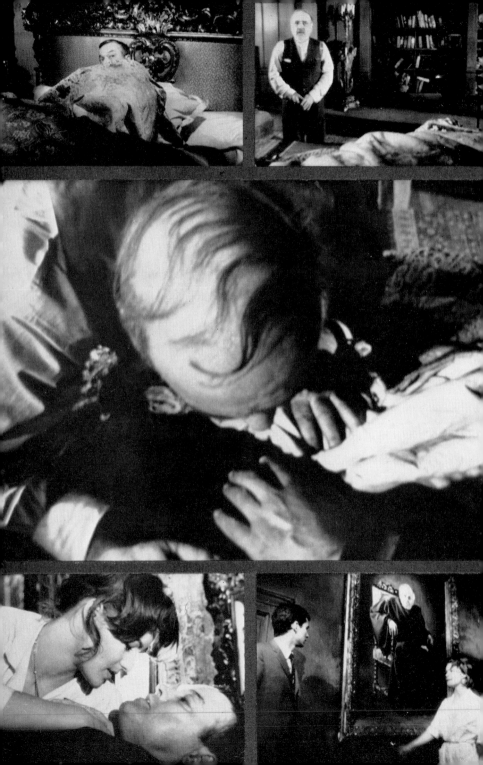

IRMIE : He keeps writing, nagging at me for news . . . he hasn't heard a thing about your case for a long time now, so naturally he's worried . . . we all are. K *has passed in front of* IRMIE.

K : Well tell him . . . not to worry.

IRMIE : Gee, I gotta write something . . . just something.

> K *starts to sit down on the stone parapet at the side of the steps.*
>
> *508. Medium shot of* K *sitting down,* IRMIE *standing on the steps behind him.*

K : Tell him everything's under control.

IRMIE : But is it?

K : I don't know . . . I . . . *He twists his handkerchief nervously.*

IRMIE : I hate to be a drag but you know what he's like . . . how he carries on about things? Now it's the honour of the family and all that jazz.

K : Maybe he's right.

IRMIE : Don't talk crap Joseph.

> *He gets up indignantly.* IRMIE *steps onto the parapet.*
>
> *509. Low angle long shot of the two of them,* IRMIE *facing camera,* K *in back view in the foreground.*

K : What? Irmie, I . . . I hope you didn't say what I thought I just heard. Aren't you ashamed to talk like that at your age? How old are you anyway?

IRMIE : Sixteen, more or less.

> *510. High angle medium close-up of* K *as seen by* IRMIE.

K : You're fifteen. Yes you are. In any case you should never have come here all by yourself.

> *511. Reverse shot of* IRMIE *as seen by* K *from below.*

IRMIE : Well, I wouldn't be here if my cousin hadn't got himself in trouble with the law.

> *512. As* K *begins to speak, cut to low angle medium shot of the two of them,* IRMIE *standing on the parapet,* K *leaning against the edge of it, in back view in the foreground.*

K : Don't they check up on you in that school?

IRMIE : They try to.

K : You sneak out after hours, is that it?

> *513. A longer shot of the two of them.* K *turns and wipes his hands with his handkerchief.*

IRMIE : You're not the only crook in the family.

K : Oh, that's not a very funny joke Irmie.

IRMIE : Okay, you write home and say what a delinquent I am. *She jumps down from the parapet.*

> *514. Low angle medium close-up of K mopping his forehead with his handkerchief,* IRMIE *in the background.*

IRMIE : But what do I say about you? There must be some kind of news?

K : Well, I . . . I'm thinking very seriously of getting rid of your father's old school chum, you can tell him that. I can't see that the famous advocate Hastler is doing anything for me except encourage the delay.

IRMIE : But he's your lawyer . . . how can you get rid of your lawyer?

K : Easy, just dismiss him from the case.

IRMIE : And . . . and then what?

K : I don't know. *He walks away.*

> *515. Long shot of the ornamental façade of the court building. At the foot of the first flight of steps,* K *walks away,* IRMIE *hurrying after him.*

IRMIE : Isn't there something more definite I can write home about?

K : No, nothing definite.

IRMIE : But you gotta have a lawyer, don't you?

K : Influence — that's all that counts in the long run. Oh, Hastler's always bragging . . .

> *516. Medium shot of K from above, back to camera, walking around between the flights of steps.* IRMIE *is following him. (Still on page 80)*

K : . . . about his personal connections, but what's he really up to? *He stops and turns to face* IRMIE. Besides I'm not exactly stupid . . .

> *517. As* K *continues, cut to a long shot of an open space surrounded by tall modern buildings, where they seem to have arrived from the law courts without transition. In the foreground on the right is the office where* K *works.*

K : . . . I can defend myself . . . look at the position I've got at the office. Don't be surprised if you hear any day now that I've become Deputy Manager of my entire department! *He walks towards the building, followed by* IRMIE. Why, all I've got to do is apply those same abilities to this case of mine. Once I get rid of the Advocate

I can draw up my own plan and keep after the officials myself.
Well . . .

518. *Low angle medium shot of* K *as he goes up the steps to
the building.* IRMIE *appears hurrying after him.*

K : . . . this is where I leave you Irmie.

IRMIE : You're not going to work now are you?

K *turning round, then pausing at the top of the steps* : Things keep
piling up — this case is taking such a lot of my time. I've really
got to finish my work somehow. I don't like to leave you alone, I
really ought to walk you back to your school.

519. *Low angle reverse shot of* IRMIE, *another vast modern
building behind her. (Still on page 80)*

IRMIE : That's all I need — for them to see me with a man.

520. *Low angle medium shot of* K, IRMIE's *head in back view
in the foreground.*

K : But I'm your cousin.

521. *Resume on* IRMIE *in low angle medium close-up.*

IRMIE : Cousins get married.

522. *Low angle long shot of* K *on top of the steps,* IRMIE *at
the bottom, back to camera.*

K : You wouldn't want to marry a criminal.

IRMIE : Crooks get married too. *They turn and walk in opposite
directions.*

523. *Medium shot of* K *going into the office building.*

K *turning and waving* : So long Irmie.

524. *Low angle medium shot of* IRMIE, *back to camera, walking
away.*

IRMIE *without turning* : So long Joseph. *Fade out.*

[[1]*We see* K *walking through his office. It is late at night and
he is alone. In a luminous island surrounded by a vast sea of
empty desks he works, or tries to, or imagines that he is
working. Finally he cannot wait any longer. He gets up and
walks across the empty office to the far corridor which contains
the electronic brain . . . sleeping in the darkness. A pool of*

---

[1] This long scene in square brackets was shot in its entirety although, as
was foreseen before the shooting started, it was cut in the final editing.
Katina Paxinou does not therefore appear in the film, although her name is
included in the credits. What follows is taken from Welles's own script.

119

light from a single bulb shows the SCIENTIST *in charge: a woman. She is wearing the same clothes as the men but that is all she has in common with her colleagues. The day shift all have expressionless faces. They are stereotyped technicians of no particular age. The woman in charge of the night shift is as old as the world. Immutable, vaguely disquieting, this venerable lady of science is the archetype of the priestess serving a powerful, millenary mystery.*

SCIENTIST : What are you doing here?

K : You told me to wait.

SCIENTIST *after a short silence* : I said that you could if you wanted to.

K : You said you would try to help me.

SCIENTIST : Yes . . . on condition that you gave us the data to work with . . . the coordinates.

K : I've got them . . . I've written everything down for you. First of all the crime, or whatever it is . . . that I'm accused of . . .

SCIENTIST : There are no coordinates for that . . . None . . . It is a simple hypothesis.

K : But everything depends on that . . . My god, if an electronic brain can't tell me that . . . I can believe no one . . .

SCIENTIST : Oh! . . . We have something for you.

K : About my case?

SCIENTIST : Don't mix cybernetics with good fortune . . . It's the best we can do with what you've given us so far.

K : I'm most grateful to you for everything . . . Then it's about my advocate . . . *The* SCIENTIST *smiles.* What's so funny about that?

SCIENTIST : The quibblings of lawyers are not within our province either.

K *trying to be tactful*: I see. I suppose a computer is rather like a judge. *The* SCIENTIST *smiles again, but* K *pursues his thesis.* Yes, why not? Why shouldn't an electronic brain replace a judge? That would be a great step nearer to perfection. Errors would no longer be possible and everything would become neat, clean and precise. Instead of trying to take advantage of us behind our backs the lawyers would be forced to be as exact as accountants or scientists. Imagine a tribunal working like a laboratory. Do you think that one day it'll be like that?

SCIENTIST : You don't really think we're going to start telling fortunes, do you? Let's be serious.

K : You're not going to tell me that your machine couldn't do it?

SCIENTIST : She wouldn't want to.

The SCIENTIST *pours some milk from a bottle into a saucer and puts it on the ground near the computer.*

K : I . . . er . . . I hope that's for a cat.

SCIENTIST : What?

K *laughing nervously*: That . . . that offering. *He smiles and pulls himself together as she raises towards him her aged, simian features.* Your specialists always talk about feeding. Of course, I was only trying to be funny.

SCIENTIST *interrupting*: It's your fault K.

K : Trying to be funny? *He feels at the end of his tether.*

SCIENTIST : What data have you given us? Practically none. Language — that's our problem.

She takes off her overall. Later she takes a raincoat from a peg and puts it on.

K : You're not going?

SCIENTIST : The night shift is over. *She looks at the brain.* Now she is resting.

K : But you have something to tell me.

SCIENTIST : Ah, yes. *She hands him a small piece of paper.*

K *looking at it* : What is it?

SCIENTIST : The crime you are most likely to commit.

K *irritated and nervous*: In the future? That sounds like fortune telling. *He looks at the paper.* Just a few holes! . . .

SCIENTIST : Facts based on the calculation of the probabilities.

K : But the questions I asked . . . where . . .

SCIENTIST *interrupting him* : I've told you. All that we can analyse are precise facts . . .

K : But there's no fact . . .

SCIENTIST : Then what do you expect? . . . Feed her vague imaginings and you'll get silence . . . Oh . . . One thing she can do is to count the stars for you.

K : No thanks.

SCIENTIST : A whole university of physicists would have to calculate for a year to solve a problem which she would solve in a few seconds . . .

K : But my problem? . . . It seems to be a bit beyond her powers.

The Scientist *smiles condescendingly.* K *continues.* I know . . .
You want to convince me that nothing is beyond the machine. But
she has her limitations. Surely that's what's happening in my case.

Scientist : You're the one who's limited . . . She can only resolve
what you can formulate . . . language.

K : Words . . .

Scientist : Although you can say exactly what you think . . . you
cannot even know what you want to know. *She moves away.* The
questions of legality or crime are despairingly resolved with so-
called moral values. Conscience, innocence, guilt . . . good and evil.

K : And all that's just imagination?

Scientist *turning towards him* : Well . . . there's nothing for us
in all that . . . nothing to get our teeth into. *She looks at the
electronic brain.* She is ready when you are, but not before . . .
*She puts her hand on the machine. It is not a familiar gesture
but rather one of respect and even a sort of pride.* She is waiting
. . . always . . .

> *She turns out the lamp. A small light continues to flash in the
> machine.* K *follows the* Scientist *as she walks away. He is
> half way down the corridor when he hears a muffled groan
> and stops. He turns his head slowly towards the source of the
> noise — the cloakroom. After a moment's indecision he comes
> and opens the door.*

Man in Leather *to* K : Mister . . .

> *The scene is exactly as* K *left it previously: the* Man in
> Leather, *the two assistant inspectors with sticking plaster
> over their mouths . . .* K *slams the door and starts to run
> across the vast open space of the office. In the next image we
> see* K *emerging from the building. Far ahead of him he sees
> the* Scientist, *who notices him and stops.* K *calls after her.*

K : What does the piece of paper say?

Scientist : I told you . . .

K *interrupting her* : It's in code or something of the sort. You
haven't translated it for me. What is it?

> *She replies at the same time as he speaks but he doesn't hear
> what she says.*

Scientist : As usual.

K : You mentioned the crime I would be most likely to commit . . .

Scientist : That's right . . . Suicide . . . *She moves away.*

K : But that's ridiculous . . . ridiculous. *He starts to follow her, but she has disappeared.*]

525. *Fade in to long shot of the corridor outside the* ADVOCATE'S *apartment. Theme music.* K *comes slowly up to the door and knocks loudly.*
526. *Close-up of the judas opening. A man's eyes appear. (Still on page 113) The judas closes.*
527. *Medium long shot of the door from the inside.* BLOCH, *the man who* K *saw sitting on a stool in a small room on his previous visit, is standing looking out through the judas.* LENI *runs up wearing only her petticoat.*
BLOCH *in a hoarse whisper* : It's him. *He opens the door.*
LENI *runs towards camera, (Still on page 113) which tracks out in front of her as* K *comes in through the door and tries to follow her. Fast jazz.* BLOCH *bars the way.* K *pushes him. Camera tilts up as* LENI *goes off, then down again to show the two men.*
K *roughly* : Who are you?
BLOCH : My name is Bloch.
K *trying to get past him* : Are you employed here?
BLOCH *holding him back* : No. I'm only a client. I don't belong to the house, I'm just here on business.
Camera tracks back in front of them as BLOCH, *holding a candle, proceeds with* K *into the* ADVOCATE'S *study.*
K *suspiciously* : In your shirtsleeves?
BLOCH *in the doorway* : Excuse me, please.
Still tracking, camera pans to show them from behind as K *follows* BLOCH *into the room and goes over to the* ADVOCATE'S *desk. The large painting of the judge, which we saw in the room full of old files, is hanging on the wall above it.*
K *accusingly* : What have you been doing . . . making love to Leni?
BLOCH *backing away from him* : No! . . . No! . . . No! . . . No!
K *simultaneously* : Well anyway you look like an honest man. What did you say your name was? Bloch?
BLOCH *backing round behind the desk* : Yes. Bloch.
K *to* BLOCH *as he scuttles off to the right* : Is that your real name?
BLOCH *scuttling back again* : Of course, why shouldn't it be?

123

K *sits down at the desk and leafs through some files.*

K : I don't know, you might have some . . . you might have some reason for concealing it.

> BLOCH *comes round behind him, watching in alarm. K slams a file shut, turns and indicates the picture hanging on the wall.*

K : You know who that is? *He gets up.*

BLOCH : Yes . . . a judge.

K : A judge of the High Court?

BLOCH *respectfully, looking up at the painting* : Oh yes, it must be.

K : That shows how much you know about the courts. Among the judges that's the lowest of the low.

BLOCH *eagerly* : Oh yes, yes, yes, of course, now I remember . . . I've been told about that before.

K : You've been told all about that before, of course you have.

BLOCH : Yes sir, I've been told this. *He backs round in front of K and off to the left.*

K *following him* : Where is she now?

> 528. *Sideways tracking shot of* LENI *running along the corridor and putting on a white overall as she goes. She is seen reflected in a series of mirrors.*

K *off* : Come on, where is Leni? Where is she hiding?

> 529. *Medium shot of the two men silhouetted behind a glass partition.*

BLOCH *backing away from* K : Leni? I don't think she's hiding, sir. She must be in the kitchen . . . Yes that's where she must be. Yes she must be in the kitchen . . . *He comes through a door in the partition followed by* K . . . making soup for the Advocate.

> *Camera tracks out slightly as* K *moves forward and grips* BLOCH *by the arm.*

K : Why didn't you tell me that before?

BLOCH : I was going to take you there, sir.

K *threateningly* : Don't think you're being clever.

BLOCH *anxiously* : Oh no, I don't, I don't think I'm clever at all. *He comes towards camera and goes off left.*

K *following him* : Lead the way then.

> 530. *Medium shot of the two men in the corridor.* BLOCH *hesitates.* K *pushes him.*

K : Go on.

Camera tracks sideways, then pans left to follow them into the kitchen which is a vast room, relatively dark like the other rooms in the apartment, with lighted candles on every piece of furniture. LENI is at one end of the room cooking at a stove. As they enter she turns and greets K.

LENI : Good evening Joseph.

BLOCH goes up to her, still holding his candle.

BLOCH *pleading* : Leni . . . um . . .

531. Medium shot of the three of them, slight high angle. K is nearest to the camera in three-quarter rear view; LENI is at her stove in profile, while BLOCH stands facing camera behind her. LENI dismisses him with a jerk of her head, and he shambles pathetically across to a chair in the corner and sits down.

K : Who's that man?

LENI *without looking at him* : His name is Bloch.

K : You were in your nightgown. *She does up a button on her overall and smoothes her hair.* Is he your lover? I want an answer.

LENI *in an undertone* : Come to the study and I'll tell you about it.

Camera pans left as K walks past LENI a little way towards BLOCH.

K : No . . . no, I want you to tell me in here.

Camera tracks in as LENI goes towards K.

LENI : You aren't jealous of poor little Bloch? You can see what he is — nothing. I just have to pay a little . . .

532. Reverse angle medium shot of the two of them, slightly from below. Standing behind K, LENI puts her arms round his waist.

LENI : . . . attention to him because he's one of the Advocate's . . .

533. Close-up of the two of them.

LENI : . . . best clients.

K looks suspiciously towards BLOCH, then bends over LENI as she kisses him and laughs. Camera tilts down with them. (Still on page 113)

534. Medium shot of BLOCH sitting pathetically in his corner, silently watching them. (Still on page 113)

535. Resume on LENI and K, in close-up, slightly from above.

LENI : You're going to spend the night with me.

125

K : The eggs are burning. LENI *disengages herself.*

536. Low angle long shot of the kitchen. LENI goes to the stove while K comes towards camera, looking at BLOCH off-screen.

LENI : Just as well — eggs are bad for him. *She turns from the stove.* If you really want to see the Advocate . . .

537. Medium shot of BLOCH sitting in his corner.

LENI *continues off* : . . . I'll tell him you're here. He's been asking after you.

538. Resume on long shot (as 536). K stands in medium shot, hands on hips.

K *turning to* LENI : Yeah, I'll bet he has. LENI *comes up to* K.

LENI : Where have you been all this time? I've got some information for you too — things I've found out. But first let's get off that jacket. *She takes off his jacket.* Shall I announce you or give him his soup first?

She walks back to the stove carrying his jacket.

K : Give him his soup. He'll need it by the time I'm through with him.

539. A high shot of BLOCH with K in the foreground.

BLOCH *to* K : So you are one of the Advocate's clients?

K *roughly* : What's that got to do with you?

540. Reverse angle medium shot of LENI on the other side of the room. She picks up a tray and turns towards them.

LENI : You be quiet, Rudy!

541. Resume on long shot (as 538).

LENI : I'll give him his soup now, but there's a chance he'll fall asleep right afterwards.

K : What I have to say to him will keep him awake.

LENI : Just as soon as he's finished eating, I'll announce you . . . I want to get you back with me. *She goes out of the room.*

542. High angle medium long shot of BLOCH sitting in his corner, K standing in back view in the foreground. A clock is heard ticking off. BLOCH makes as if to get up as we hear LENI's receding footsteps off.

K *curtly* : Keep your seat!

Camera tracks in as K goes up to him and sits down beside him.

K *continues* : So! You're . . . you're one of the Advocate's clients?

BLOCH : Oh yes . . . yes, a very old client indeed.

543. Close-up of the two of them, BLOCH *in three-quarter back view,* K *three-quarters facing camera.*

K : How long's he been in charge of your affairs for?

BLOCH : Affairs?

544. Reverse shot with BLOCH *three-quarters facing camera.*

BLOCH : Business affairs! *He chuckles.* Oh! He's been my representative since . . . hm . . . the very beginning . . . hm . . . but my case . . . K *nods.*

545. Medium close-up of the two of them from the side. At the word ' case ' BLOCH *suddenly springs to life. He puts his candlestick on a nearby shelf and rummages in his hip pocket.*

BLOCH : That's what — probably — you were thinking about. I've got it all written down here. *He takes a small notebook out of his pocket and flips through it feverishly.* I can give you the exact dates. Now . . . it's very difficult to keep all that in one's head so I'm . . .

K *interrupting him* : Oh I didn't . . . I didn't . . . I never realised that Hastler had an ordinary commercial practice as well.

BLOCH *tucking the book into a pocket in his waistcoat* : Of course. Why . . .

546. Close-up of the two of them, BLOCH *three-quarters facing camera.*

BLOCH : . . . yes, you know that they even say . . . *He leans forward confidentially (Still on page 113)* . . . they even say that he's a better advocate for . . .

547. Reverse angle close-up, K *three-quarters facing camera.*

BLOCH : . . . business — right? — than for the other kind.

K : Yes?

BLOCH : Oh yes.

548. Reverse shot (as 546).

BLOCH *anxiously* : You won't give me away?

549. Low angle medium close-up of them from the side (as 545).

K : I'm not an informer.

BLOCH *leaning forward* : He's a revengeful man . . . very, very revengeful.

K *shifting in his chair* : Why surely he wouldn't . . . he wouldn't think of harming one of his own clients?

BLOCH *vehemently*: Yes! Yes!

> *550. Close-up of the two of them,* BLOCH *three-quarters facing camera.*

BLOCH: Yes, once he's roused, he'll do anything. He doesn't draw any distinctions.

> *551. Reverse shot,* K *three-quarters facing camera,* BLOCH *in the foreground.*

K: What . . . what was it you wanted to tell me?

> *552. Reverse shot (as 550).*

BLOCH: You'll have to tell me one of your own secrets. Please. *He drops his voice.* So we can trust each other . . .

> *553. Medium close-up of the two of them in profile.*

BLOCH: . . . to keep quiet.

K *smiling ironically*: Okay, okay, I'll give you a secret.

BLOCH: Then I have . . . *A pause. He looks round nervously, then brings his chair closer to K and speaks in his ear* . . . I have other advocates.

K *smiling again*: Other . . . other advocates?

> *554. Close-up of them,* K *in three-quarter back view,* BLOCH *facing.*

K: . . . as well as Hastler?

BLOCH *holding up five fingers*: Five of them.

> *555. Reverse shot,* K *facing. They both laugh.*
>
> *556. Reverse shot (as 554).*

BLOCH *laughing*: You know . . . *He laughs heartily.* Hastler . . .

> *557. Close-up of the two of them laughing (as 555).*
>
> *558. Medium close-up of them in profile, low angle.*

BLOCH: . . . Listen . . .

K: Yeah?

BLOCH: . . . Hastler, yes, is always ref . . . K *laughs uncontrollably.*

> *559. Close-up of them,* BLOCH *facing.* K *continues to laugh.*

BLOCH: Wait a minute, wait a minute . . . Hastler . . .

> *560. Reverse shot,* K *facing.*

BLOCH: . . . he's always referring to the others in his own circle as . . .

> *561. Reverse shot (as 559).* BLOCH *taps himself on the chest and imitates the voice of the* ADVOCATE.

BLOCH: . . . 'great advocates'. *He makes a disgusted face.* Bah!

K *laughs.*

562. Reverse shot (as 560)

K *in disbelief*: No!

BLOCH *disgustedly*: Yes!

K *laughing*: No!

BLOCH: Yes . . . But in the real protocol of the court . . .

K: Yeah?

563. Close-up of BLOCH *leaning towards* K, *who is in three-quarter back view.*

BLOCH: . . . he ranks where?

K: Where?

BLOCH *disdainfully*: Among the small advocates. Oh sure!

K: Hastler?

BLOCH: Uh huh! Why the really great advocates, who are never seen, must . . .

564. As K *breaks in, cut to reverse shot,* K *facing camera.*

K: Then you must have been working on your own behalf?

BLOCH: Oh yes.

K: You know, I'd like to ask you about that.

BLOCH: Ah?

K: How do you do that?

BLOCH: It's exhausting . . .

565. Reverse shot (as 563). BLOCH *leans towards* K *again.*

BLOCH: Just attending the court to try to keep an eye on things . . . Too much for one man.

566. Reverse shot (as 564).

BLOCH: Mmm.

K: I'll be there often enough myself after this, I suppose.

BLOCH: Oh! Ah!

K: I can't expect the same special treatment I got that first time. Everybody stood up. They must have taken me for a judge. BLOCH *chuckles.*

567. Reverse shot, BLOCH *facing.*

BLOCH: It was that guard you were with. He was the one we all stood up for.

568. Medium long shot of LENI *arriving by the portrait in the* ADVOCATE's *study with her tray.*

BLOCH *off*: There's that ridiculous superstition . . .

569. Resume on close-up of the two men, BLOCH *in three-*

quarter back view, K *three-quarters facing camera.*

K : What superstition?

BLOCH : You're supposed to be able to tell . . .

570. Reverse shot, BLOCH *facing.*

BLOCH : . . . from a man's face . . . and from the line of his lips . . .

571. Reverse shot (as 569).

BLOCH : . . . especially . . . how his case is going to turn out.

K *anxiously* : So?

572. Reverse shot (as 570).

BLOCH : So, the people are saying that from the expression on your lips they could tell that . . . *He pauses and looks up at* K . . . you'd be found guilty.

573. Reverse shot, K *facing. He looks horrified.*

BLOCH : Yes, in the very near future.

574. Medium shot of LENI *by the portrait with the tray.*

LENI *to* K : The Advocate is waiting for you.

575. Long shot of the two men getting up, surprised at LENI'S *unexpected appearance.*

K *irritated* : Let him wait.

LENI *off* : You can talk to Bloch later.

576. Resume on LENI.

LENI : He's sleeping here.

K *off, in surprise* : Sleeping here?

LENI *coming forward with her tray and addressing* K : Everybody isn't like you — expecting to be granted an interview at any hour of the day or night. *As she speaks, camera pans left to follow her as she goes and puts down her tray on a sideboard.* And the Advocate sick as he is, too. *Camera pans left again, then tracks in behind her as she goes up to the two men.* Your friends do you favours and you just take them for granted. *She moves between* K *and* BLOCH, *drawing* K *lovingly to one side. Camera pans left with them, cutting out* BLOCH. Not that I ask for any thanks. All I want . . . well . . . *She stops and looks up at him* . . . I want you to be fond of me.

K *petulantly* : I'm fond of you. Well, I don't know. Why shouldn't Hastler be willing to see me? He's my lawyer isn't he? What kind of a favour is that? *He moves away as* BLOCH *appears on the right.*

577. High angle close-up of BLOCH, *three-quarters facing camera,* LENI *in profile on the left. (Still on page 113)*

130

BLOCH : That's not the point.

LENI : Rudi, you can see he's just being disagreeable.

They look at each other for a moment.

BLOCH : You know why the Advocate is . . .

578. *Close-up of* LENI's *face, turned towards* BLOCH, *who is in the foreground;* K *is partly visible in the background.*

BLOCH : . . . seeing him Leni? I'll tell you. It's because . . .

579. *Resume on close-up of* BLOCH *(as 577).*

BLOCH : . . . his case is still at the hopeful stage. Oh yes, Leni . . .

580. *Medium shot of the three of them.* LENI *is between the two men, facing* BLOCH. *She buttons up his waistcoat as he speaks.*

BLOCH : He'll see. Later it'll be different.

LENI : You talk too much. *She turns towards* K *and buttons up his waistcoat as she addresses him.* That's his trouble. That's why the Advocate can't bear to see him.

BLOCH : Oh . . . Oh, he does see me occasionally. But you never know. That's what's so . . .

581. *Close-up of* LENI's *face. She looks up at* K.

BLOCH *off* : . . . nerve . . .

582. *High angle close-up of* LENI's *hand, doing up and undoing the same button on* K's *waistcoat.*

BLOCH *continuing, off* : . . . wracking.

583. *Close-up of* LENI *with* K's *chest in the background. She looks at* BLOCH, *in the foreground, as the latter continues.*

BLOCH : You never know when he'll be willing to receive you.

584. *High angle close-up of* LENI's *hand fiddling with* K's *waistcoat button. Camera tilts up to show* K's *nervous face.*

BLOCH *off* : It could be any time — day, night — and if I'm not right here on the spot when he does take it into his head . . .

585. *Close-up of* BLOCH, *the top half of* LENI's *face in foreground.*

BLOCH : . . . to send for me . . . Hah! I've lost my chance. Hmm. *Camera tilts down slightly, showing the whole of* LENI's *face as* BLOCH *continues miserably.* Then I have to wait much longer than before.

LENI : That's why I let you sleep here. *She turns as* K *speaks, off.*

K *off* : Well I guess . . .

586. *Close-up of* K's *face. He speaks thoughtfully.*

K : . . . one gets very dependent on one's advocate as time goes on.

587. Close-up of LENI's *face in profile, between the two men.*

LENI : The truth is, he likes it. *She looks up at* BLOCH.

588. Reverse angle close-up of BLOCH *facing camera,* K *back to camera,* LENI *in profile between them.*

BLOCH *imploring* : Leni . . .

LENI : Maybe not the waiting . . . But you do enjoy spending the night . . . now don't you ? Good.

589. Close-up of K's *face. He looks thoughtful.*

590. High angle close-up of LENI's *face,* K's *shoulder in foreground.*

LENI *to* K *in a whisper* : Want to see his room ?

591. Resume on K. *He opens his mouth but says nothing.*

592. High angle close-up of LENI, *watching* K, *and* BLOCH, *watching* LENI.

593. Resume on close-up of K's *face.*

K *nervously, almost in a whisper* : Okay.

594. High angle close-up of LENI's *face as she looks tenderly up at* K, *who is partly visible in left foreground.*

595. High angle close-up of the three of them. K *turns and they move off,* BLOCH *last.*

596. Medium shot: camera pans slightly left as LENI, *flanked by the two men, arrives at the doorway of* BLOCH's *room. (Still on page 113)*

597. High angle reverse shot of what they see: the tiny room with a bed and a small circular window. (Still on page 113)

K *quietly, off* : So you sleep in the maid's room ?

598. Low angle medium close-up of them in the doorway.

BLOCH : Yes, she let's me have it, yes . . . it . . . it's very convenient. *Music.* LENI *turns to* BLOCH. *A pause. Then she sighs and tilts her head backwards, resting it on* K's *shoulder. The two men look at each other. A pause.*

K *curtly* : Put him to bed.

599. High angle close-up of the three of them. K *removes his shoulder, turns and walks away.* BLOCH *hurries after him.*

BLOCH : Mr. K, wait !

600. Medium shot of BLOCH *hurrying after* K *as he goes out through the doorway.*

BLOCH : Wait, Mr. K !

LENI *trying to pull him back* : Rudy!

> *601. Low angle long shot of one of the vast rooms in the apartment. K enters at the back and strides towards camera, followed by* BLOCH *and* LENI.

BLOCH *pleading*: Mr. K! Mr. K! K *halts in medium shot as* BLOCH *comes round in front of him, back to camera.* Please! You've forgotten your promise. You . . . you were going to tell me one of your secrets.

K : All right I'll give you a secret. *A pause.* I'm dismissing the Advocate.

> BLOCH *starts forward.*

LENI *in surprise* : The Advocate?

BLOCH *dumbfounded* : What?

K : I'm going to dismiss him from my case.

> K *walks towards camera, which tracks backwards, tilted up towards him, as he passes through several rooms in the apartment.* LENI *and* BLOCH *follow him in alarm, trying to stop him and dissuade him from his mad idea.*

BLOCH : Dismiss him from your case?

K *simultaneously* : I'm tired of all these delays. Hastler's done nothing.

LENI : Please, no, you can't!

K : He's either too old, too sick or too indifferent!

BLOCH *indignantly* : Dismiss the Advocate!

LENI : Please, no . . . he's not indifferent.

BLOCH : He's dismissing the Advocate!

LENI : Wait, no, please . . . don't.

> *Camera halts as they arrive under the painting of the judge.* LENI *throws her arms round* K *in order to stop him.* BLOCH *intervenes,* K *struggles to get free.* LENI *screams.* BLOCH *grunts.* K *retreats through a doorway followed by* LENI, *who is still hanging onto him.*
>
> *602. Long shot of the two of them seen from the end of the corridor which leads into the* ADVOCATE'S *bedroom.* LENI *lets go of* K *and locks the door behind her to keep* BLOCH *out.*

LENI *to* BLOCH : Aaah! You stay out!

> *Camera pans left as she pursues* K *along the corridor, gasping, trying to hold him back. Finally she kicks him on the ankle.*

K : Ow!

603. *Long shot of the* ADVOCATE'S *bedroom.* LENI *crosses frame, followed by K nursing his injured ankle. He mounts the platform on which the* ADVOCATE'S *bed stands.*

ADVOCATE : Leave him alone Leni. *He chuckles.*

604. *Medium close-up of the* ADVOCATE *as seen by K.*

ADVOCATE : Has she been pestering you again?

605. *Reverse angle medium shot of* K *as seen by the* ADVOCATE.

K : Pestering me?

ADVOCATE : She finds all . . .

606. *Resume on him (as 604).*

ADVOCATE : . . . accused men attractive.

607. *Low angle medium close-up of* K *against the window. He looks puzzled as the* ADVOCATE *continues off.*

ADVOCATE : It's a . . .

608. *Slight high angle close-up of the* ADVOCATE *looking up at* K *off-screen.*

ADVOCATE : . . . peculiarity of hers. She makes up to all of them — makes love to all of them . . . and when I allow her to, she tells me about these affairs, to amuse me. All about them.

609. *Resume on* K *in low angle medium close-up.*

ADVOCATE *off* : You came here this evening . . .

610. *Resume on the* ADVOCATE *in medium close-up, slight high angle.*

ADVOCATE : . . . for a specific reason?

K *off* : Yes.

611. *Resume on* K *(as 609).*

K : I came here to tell you that I'm dispensing with your services.

612. *High angle medium shot of the* ADVOCATE *in bed. We see the back of* K's *head just in front of the camera.*

ADVOCATE : You mustn't be in too much of a hurry.

K : I know you've done everything you can for me, and . . .

613. *Low angle medium shot of* K.

K : . . . I appreciate it, but I'm afraid that more energetic steps are going to have to be taken.

614. *Resume on the* ADVOCATE.

ADVOCATE : Huh! That's a plan we can discuss.

615. *Resume on* K *(as 613).*

K : It's not a plan . . . it's a fact.

616. Rapid close-up of the ADVOCATE *gazing silently up at* K.

617. Resume on K *in low angle medium close-up.*

K : How many times have I come here? And what have you done for me? Nothing!

618. Resume on the ADVOCATE *(as 616).*

ADVOCATE : How many of my clients have reached the same point in their cases as you? . . .

619. Resume on K.

ADVOCATE *continuing, off*: . . . And stood here before me saying . . .

620. Resume on the ADVOCATE.

ADVOCATE : . . . exactly the same things.

K : Maybe they had . . .

621. Resume on K.

K : . . . a reason to. They were probably all just as much in the right as I am.

622. High angle close-up of the ADVOCATE.

ADVOCATE : It's true you know. *A pause. He continues slowly.* Accused men *are* attractive.

623. Resume on K. *He listens, slightly puzzled.*

ADVOCATE *off*: Not that being accused immediately shows in a man's personal appearance . . .

624. Resume on the ADVOCATE *(as 622).*

ADVOCATE : But if you've got the right eye for these things, you can pick out an accused man in the largest crowd. There's just something . . .

625. Back to K.

ADVOCATE *off*: . . . about them. Something . . .

626. Back to the ADVOCATE.

ADVOCATE *after a pause*: . . . attractive. It can't be a sense of guilt. We can't all be . . . guilty. Hmmm? Some, of course, are more attractive than others but all are attractive, even that wretched creature Bloch. *Grimly.* Let's get him in here.

627. A longer shot of K *at the foot of the bed in the fore-ground.*

ADVOCATE *off*: I think it's time you learnt how other accused men are treated. Get Bloch . . .

628. Resume on the ADVOCATE *in medium close-up.*

ADVOCATE : . . . in here, Leni!

629. Low angle medium close-up of LENI, *who has been*

standing, listening. She starts as the ADVOCATE *addresses her.*
630. Low angle medium close-up of K. *He looks towards* LENI.
ADVOCATE *off* : Go . . .
    631. High angle close-up of the ADVOCATE.
ADVOCATE : . . . and fetch Bloch !
    632. Long shot of the room. Camera tracks in towards the bed as LENI *goes off and* K *moves to the left. Music. The* ADVOCATE *lies back and draws the sheet up over his face.*
    633. Medium shot of K *walking round the side of the bed behind a screen. Camera tracks in as he looks down at the* ADVOCATE.
K : My decision is final you know.
    634. High angle close-up of the ADVOCATE *in bed.*
ADVOCATE : You'd better think about it Joseph. *He draws the sheet up over his face.*
    635. Resume on medium shot of the two of them (as 633). The ADVOCATE *draws the screen across.*
    636. Low angle reverse shot from the other side of the bed. As the ADVOCATE *moves the screen across,* K *turns and walks away.*
    637. High angle close-up of the ADVOCATE *looking out from under the sheet.*
LENI *to* BLOCH *off* : The Advocate wants to see you.
    638. Long shot of the corridor outside the bedroom. At the far end LENI *ushers in* BLOCH.
    639. Medium long shot of K *standing by a filing system. He turns.*
    640. Resume on the corridor. Overcome with joy, BLOCH *hurries into the room, followed by* LENI. *Music.*
LENI : Go on.
BLOCH : Oh thank you, thank you.
    The camera tracks left to follow him as he hurries to the edge of the bed platform, where the ADVOCATE *is lying with the sheet over his face.*
ADVOCATE *hidden by the bedclothes* : Is that Bloch?
BLOCH *nervously* : Yes . . . yes, sir.
ADVOCATE *roughly* : What do you want? *Silence.* You were sent for weren't you?
BLOCH *confused* : Yes sir, I was.

ADVOCATE *in the same hectoring tone* : You've come at the wrong
time !
BLOCH : But sir, I came immediately . . . immediately, sir — the
minute I heard my name. *A pause.* Do you want me to go away?
ADVOCATE *snarling at him* : You're here aren't you?
BLOCH : Yes, sir, I . . . I'm here . . . I . . . *A pause.*
ADVOCATE : Then stay.
BLOCH : Ye . . . yes.
ADVOCATE : Yesterday . . .
    641. High angle medium close-up of the ADVOCATE *raising the
sheet slightly. His eyes watch* BLOCH *coldly. (Still on page 114)*
ADVOCATE : . . . I saw my friend the Third Judge.
    642. Medium long shot of K *standing by the index system,
listening.*
ADVOCATE *continuing off* : I managed to work . . .
    643. Medium shot of BLOCH *at the front of the bed, as seen by
the* ADVOCATE.
ADVOCATE *off* : . . . the conversation round to your case.
BLOCH *eagerly* : My case !
ADVOCATE *off* : You want to hear what he said?
BLOCH *imploring* : Oh please !
    644. Medium close-up of the ADVOCATE *sitting up in bed.*
ADVOCATE : In these matters there are so many conflicting opinions
that the confusion is . . .
    645. Resume on BLOCH, *standing nervously at the foot of the
bed. (Still on page 114) The* ADVOCATE *continues off.*
ADVOCATE : . . . impenetrable. At a certain point, by an old
tradition, a bell must be rung.
BLOCH *nodding eagerly* : Oh yes, a bell.
ADVOCATE *off* : The judge holds that this marks the official opening
of the proceedings.
    646. A closer shot of the ADVOCATE.
ADVOCATE : There are many arguments against this opinion, but
you wouldn't understand them.
    647. Resume on BLOCH. *He kneels down.* K *leaps into frame
from the right, followed by* LENI, *and a violent struggle ensues.*
BLOCH : Yes sir.
    K *tries to yank* BLOCH *to his feet but* BLOCH *pushes him aside.*
LENI *drags* K *back.*

K *disgustedly* : What are you doing on your knees?

LENI *simultaneously, screaming* : No! No! No!

ADVOCATE *shouting, off* : Who is your advocate?

BLOCH *desperately* : You! You!

> *648. Resume on the* ADVOCATE *in medium close-up.*

ADVOCATE : And beside me?

> *649. Resume on* BLOCH, *still on his knees. On the right,* LENI *is still restraining* K.

BLOCH : No-one sir, no-one!

> *650. Resume on the* ADVOCATE.

ADVOCATE : Then pay no attention to anyone else.

> *651. Reverse shot:* K *leans over* BLOCH, *still restrained by* LENI.

K *contemptuously* : Crawl on the floor then if you like!

BLOCH : No! no!

> *652. Medium close-up of the* ADVOCATE. *He lies back and covers his face again.*

BLOCH *to* K *off* : You're not to talk to me like that!

> *653. Medium shot of the other three.* BLOCH *gets up and starts hitting* K, *who hits him back.* LENI *clings to* K *and screams.*

BLOCH : Not in front of the Advocate! How dare you! How dare you! How dare you ... insult me! ...

> *654. Reverse angle medium shot, the bed in the background.*

BLOCH : ... in front of the Advocate!

> K *stands, restraining* LENI *with one hand and holding* BLOCH *at arm's length with the other.*

K *to* BLOCH : Don't you see?

> *655. Medium close-up of the* ADVOCATE, *who sits up slightly and watches them.*

K *off* : He's only trying to humiliate you ...

> *656. Resume on the three of them.*

K : ... to show off his power.

> LENI *tries to bite him on the arm.*

BLOCH : You shouldn't!

> *657. Reverse shot of the three of them as seen by the* ADVOCATE. BLOCH *turns towards the bed as the latter addresses him.*

ADVOCATE *off* : Pay no attention to anyone.

LENI : Rudy!

658. Resume on the ADVOCATE.

LENI *off* : Let him go !

ADVOCATE *self-righteously* : Do what your conscience tells you is right. *He covers himself with the sheet again.*

659. Resume on the three of them as seen from the bed.

BLOCH *leaning forward anxiously* : I'm on my knees, on my knees, Advocate.

Behind him, K *struggles with* LENI, *who screams at him.*

LENI : Let me go ! *He finally throws her to the ground.*

660. Reverse angle long shot towards the bed.

BLOCH *kneeling at the foot of the bed* : I'm on my knees Advocate, I'm on my knees, sir.

LENI *gets up in the foreground and runs round to the side of the bed, in front of* BLOCH.

661. Low angle medium close-up of BLOCH, *kneeling, back to camera.* LENI *leans over him, indicating that he should kiss the* ADVOCATE'S *hand.*

BLOCH : I'm on . . . What? . . . Oh . . . *He breaks off as he realises what is required of him and crawls forward as* LENI *draws back the bedcover.*

662. Low angle medium close-up of K *watching.*

663. Low angle long shot, K *in back view on the left.* LENI *runs round to the other side of the bed.*

664. High angle close-up of BLOCH *as he uncovers the* ADVOCATE'S *hand and kisses it. (Still on page 114) We hear the sound of him doing so.*

665. Resume on K, *looking on with mingled puzzlement and disgust. He looks at* LENI *off-screen.*

666. Low angle medium shot of LENI *looking round the screen on the opposite side of the bed. We see* BLOCH'S *posterior as he bends over the* ADVOCATE'S *hand in the foreground.* LENI *motions to him to kiss it again.*

667. Resume on high angle close-up of BLOCH. *He kisses the hand again, then covers it reverently.*

668. Low angle medium shot (as 666). LENI *moves towards the bed while* BLOCH *backs away on his knees towards camera.*

669. Medium close-up of LENI *from the side as she sits down on the bed beside the* ADVOCATE.

670. Medium close-up of BLOCH *as he retreats and kneels down again at the end of the bed.* K *is seen in the background.*

671. Medium close-up of the ADVOCATE *lying in bed with* LENI *sitting beside him (as 669).* LENI *opens a bottle of liquid and shakes some into her hand.*

ADVOCATE : How's he been behaving today?

672. Medium close-up of BLOCH *(as 670). He listens anxiously.*

673. Resume on close-up of LENI *and the* ADVOCATE*. She lovingly rubs the contents of the bottle into his chin and chest. (Still on page 114)*

LENI : He's been quiet and hardworking.

ADVOCATE *taking the bottle from her* : What's he been doing all day?

LENI : I kept him locked up in the maid's room so he wouldn't disturb me in my work . . . It's where he usually stays anyway.

ADVOCATE : Then you can't say with real knowledge what he's been doing.

LENI : I peeped in on him now and then through the ventilator. He was kneeling all the time on the bed . . . studying the book you let him borrow. There wasn't much light, so the way he stuck to his reading shows that he does what he's told.

ADVOCATE : Did he understand what he was reading?

LENI : Well, he was following the lines with his fingers. All I could tell was he never goes past the same page the whole day. I guess the book is very hard to understand.

ADVOCATE *ponderously* : Yes . . . The scriptures are very difficult.

LENI *gets up.*

674. Medium shot of the bed. BLOCH *is still on his knees.*

ADVOCATE : They are only meant to give him a bare inkling . . .

BLOCH *nodding feverishly* : Yes.

Camera pans, following LENI *as she walks towards* K.

ADVOCATE : . . . of the complications I must struggle with on his behalf.

675. Medium shot of LENI *and* K *as seen by the* ADVOCATE, BLOCH *at the foot of the bed in the foreground.*

ADVOCATE *continuing* : Did he read without stopping?

LENI : Almost without stopping. Once he asked me for a drink of water and I handed it to him through the ventilator . . . Then about eight o'clock I let him out and gave him something to eat.

676. Medium shot of the ADVOCATE *sitting up again.*

ADVOCATE : You're praising him too much, Leni.

677. A medium shot (as 675): BLOCH, LENI and K.

ADVOCATE *continuing, off* : You're making it even harder for me to tell the truth.

678. Resume on the ADVOCATE in medium close-up.

ADVOCATE : The judges remarks were by no means favourable.

679. Resume on the trio.

LENI : Not favourable? How can that be?

ADVOCATE : He was even annoyed . . .

680. Resume on the ADVOCATE.

ADVOCATE : . . . when I mentioned Bloch's name — ' You're wasting you're time with that man,' he told me, ' his case is . . . hopeless '.

681. Back to the other three.

ADVOCATE *off* : ' I refuse to believe that. Bloch is most . . .'

682. Resume on the ADVOCATE.

ADVOCATE : '. . . conscientious ', I told him . . . ' It's true that personally he's rather repulsive — his manners are bad and he's dirty . . .'

683. Resume on BLOCH, crushed.

ADVOCATE *off* : '. . . But as a client ', I said, ' he's . . .'

684. Resume on the ADVOCATE.

ADVOCATE : '. . . beyond reproach.' — which was, of course, a deliberate exaggeration.

A pause.

685. Resume on BLOCH, still looking dismayed, the other two behind him.

ADVOCATE *off* : And here's what the judge replied to that : ' Your . . . your client . . . has a . . .'

686. Resume on the ADVOCATE.

ADVOCATE : '. . . kind of low cunning. He's learnt . . .'

687. Resume on BLOCH, looking more and more hang-dog, LENI and K watching behind.

ADVOCATE *off* : '. . . through the years how to go on manipulating the situation. But what do you think he'd say if we were to tell him . . .'

688. Resume on the ADVOCATE.

ADVOCATE : '. . . that the bell marking the start of the proceedings . . .' *He pauses sinisterly* '. . . hadn't even been rung? '

BLOCH *breaks into loud sobs off. The* ADVOCATE *roars at him.*

ADVOCATE : Quiet there Bloch!

689. Rapid shot of BLOCH *sobbing noisily.*

690. Resume on the ADVOCATE.

ADVOCATE : Have you no shame, to behave like that in front of my client? You're destroying his confidence in me.

691. Low angle medium close-up of K *watching.*

ADVOCATE *continuing, off* : What's wrong with you, eh?

692. Resume on the ADVOCATE.

ADVOCATE : You're still alive, aren't you?

693. Long shot of the room, slight low angle; K *is in the foreground, back to camera,* LENI *next to him,* BLOCH *on his knees at the foot of the bed, and in the background the* ADVOCATE.

ADVOCATE : You're still under my protection.

K : I hope you realise that I'm dispensing with your services.
Camera pans right as he makes angrily for the door but stops at the ADVOCATE'S *next words.*

ADVOCATE : You can still change your mind about that.

694. Resume on the ADVOCATE *in medium close-up, sitting up in bed, the prostrate* BLOCH *in the foreground.*

ADVOCATE : To be in chains is sometimes safer than to be free.

695. Low angle medium close-up of K. *He pauses, then goes out of the room, camera tilting down to follow him.*

696. Resume on the ADVOCATE *in medium close-up. He starts to laugh. His laugh echoes round the room and in the corridors outside.*

697. Medium close-up of BLOCH *looking up, and behind him* LENI, *in profile, looking after* K.

698. Low angle medium close-up of her. Camera pans as she runs after K.

699. High angle close-up of the ADVOCATE *heaving with laughter.*

700. Music in. The ADVOCATE'S *laughter echoes through the apartment as* K *strides through it, camera panning and tracking with him from a low angle. He comes face to face with* LENI *who is holding his jacket.*

LENI : Where do you think you're going?

K *roughly* : Open the door!

Camera pans as she follows him to a door beside the painting of the judge hanging on the wall.

LENI : You must be crazy!

K : Open the door!

LENI : There's no place for you to go.

The ADVOCATE *laughs louder and louder off.*

K *putting on his jacket* : He's the one who's crazy. If I hadn't made up my mind already, that performance in there would have settled it for ever. And to think it was all put on for my benefit! To win me over!

LENI : How far do you think you could get without him? *A pause.*

K *slowly* : How far am I now? . . . How far to where?

LENI *jerking her head at the painting, off-screen to the right* : You'd better see him.

K *turning and looking at the picture* : Who? The high court judge?

> *Camera pans as* LENI *moves in front of the painting. (Still on page 114)*

LENI : Don't be funny . . . of course not. *Showing him the signature on the painting.* I mean Titorelli. He's the official court painter. He knows them all. They all come to his studio to sit for their portraits. Nobody has more influence with the judges than Titorelli.

K : You really think he could help me?

> *She moves closer to K and looks up at him. Camera pans again.*

LENI : That's his profession really — as much as painting — helping people.

K *putting a hand on the door* : Unlock the door will you?

LENI : Wait till the morning.

K : Where are the keys?

LENI : The Advocate keeps the keys.

K *taking a step back* : Okay.

> *701. Medium close-up of K breaking open the door with a crash.*
>
> *702. Reverse shot of the door from outside. K bursts it open and goes off on the left.* LENI *appears in the doorway, looking after him.*

K *off* : Goodbye Leni and thanks.

LENI : You'll be back here?

K *off* : No, no.

LENI : You won't have any choice.

K *off* : No, honey, I've seen what it is to be one of his clients.

> *703. Reverse angle medium shot of the doorway.* K *stands facing* LENI.

K : I've seen what happened to Bloch. He's not a client, he's the Advocate's dog!

> *704. Medium close-up of* LENI *standing motionless.*
>
> *705. Reverse shot (as 703).* K *shuts the door.*

> *706. Dissolve to medium shot of* K *opening a door into an apartment building and walking down a dingy corridor, away from camera. Fast jazz.*
>
> *707. Low angle medium shot of* K. *He turns a bend in the corridor, meets some young girls and addresses them.*

K : Uh . . . Uh . . . Excuse me, is there a Mr. Titorelli?

> *A hunchbacked girl moves towards him.*

GIRL : Who?

K *embarrassed* : . . . Artist living here?

> *Another, blonde girl points to indicate that the painter is upstairs.*

K : You know the painter Titorelli?

> *As he speaks,* K *moves forward and off to the left.*

FIRST GIRL : What do you want him for?

> *A third girl runs after* K.

K *off* : I want him . . .

> *708. High angle medium shot of* K *going up the first few steps of a spiral staircase. In the foreground, more girls crowd through a doorway after him, yelling at his heels.*

K : . . . to paint my portrait.

A GIRL : Your portrait?

> *709. Low angle medium close-up of the two girls* K *spoke to first. They rush gleefully after him.*
>
> *710. Medium shot of the stair well from above as* K *comes up the stairs, pursued by screaming girls. Camera pans right with him.*
>
> *711. Similar shot from below:* K *surrounded by screaming girls. (Still on page 115)*
>
> *712. Another shot from above,* K's *face lit from below.*
>
> *713. A shot directly from below, looking up the stair well. The*

fast jazz continues over the screaming.

714. Low angle medium close-up of K *surrounded by girls, clutching at him and shouting. He looks faintly amused.*

715. High angle close-up of his pursuers.

716. Low angle medium shot: there are a couple of girls in front of K. *The ones behind are pulling at his jacket. (Still on page 115)*

717. Medium close-up from above. K *struggles on. Camera swivels round to follow him.*

718. Medium shot (as 716).

719. A high shot from the top of the stair well where the staircase ends in a flight of wooden steps.

720. Camera tracks out from under the wooden steps, panning right and tilting to follow K *as he climbs up.*

721. Close-up of a girl running to the foot of a ladder which runs parallel with the steps. Camera pans left then tilts up to follow her.

722. Medium shot of K *climbing the wooden steps, girls in front and behind him.*

723. High angle shot of K *running up the steps as the girl climbs the ladder beside him.*

724. Low angle medium close-up of K *climbing further. The screaming and the music continue.*

725. High angle shot of K *arriving at the top of the steps. Camera tilts up with him as a wooden door suddenly opens beside him and a strange-looking man in pyjamas,* TITORELLI, *beckons him in.*

TITORELLI : I must teach you how to deal with girls.

726. Low angle shot of the top of TITORELLI'S *studio which proves to be a dilapidated shack made from wooden slats, perched at the top of the stair well. The girls rush up the ladder and crowd round it screaming.*

TITORELLI *off* : Damned little pests! Out!

727. In the next shot we are inside TITORELLI'S *studio. Close-up of two girls peering through the slats which form the walls of the structure. (Still on page 115)*

TITORELLI *off* : Out of my . . .

728. Close-up of another girl.

TITORELLI *off* : . . . studio!

Whip pan to two more faces and slight track out.

TITORELLI : This is no time for your . . .

729. *Low angle medium shot: a child runs across the studio and flops on the bed, pursued by the painter. Slight pan right.*

TITORELLI : . . . silly games . . . This gentleman's here on business.

730. *High angle close-up of two girls' faces through the planks.*

731. *Resume on the painter as he carries the child bodily to the door. Others rush in behind him and descend on K.*

TITORELLI : Out . . .

732. *Low angle medium shot of the outside of the shack. The door flies open and a child exits backwards.*

TITORELLI *off* : . . . you wretches get . . .

733. *Medium close-up of the door from the outside as TITORELLI shuts it. The girls crowd round.*

TITORELLI : . . . out!

734. *Close-up of the faces behind the slats.*

TITORELLI *off* : Why can't you play . . .

735. *Low angle close-up of K standing in the middle of the studio. (Still on page 115)*

TITORELLI *off* : . . . in somebody else's . . .

736. *Close-up of another face, other girls dancing around behind it. (Still on page 115)*

TITORELLI *off* : . . . studio? . . . Or stay at home?

737. *Close-up of two more faces.*

738. *Low angle medium shot of the studio. K stands watching on the right as TITORELLI rushes across to one of the gaps in the wall.*

TITORELLI : Oh . . . I can see you!

739. *Jump cut to close-up of another girl's face. The screaming dies down.*

740. *Resume on low angle close-up of K. He glances nervously to and fro.*

741. *Close-up of another face, one eye visible.*

742. *Resume on K. He glances sideways.*

743. *Close-up of two more faces, watching him through the slats.*

744. *Jump cut to K. He looks to the right.*

745. *Jump cut to another face.*

746. *Close-up. Sound of whispering. Camera pans right with*

another face.

TITORELLI *off* : I can . . .

747. *Close-up of an eye looking through the slats. It moves across and is replaced by the other eye of the same face. (Still on page 115)*

TITORELLI *off* : . . . see you. Don't think you're fooling Titorelli.

748. *Resume on* K. *Girlish shrieks off. He looks nervously down at the slats.*

749. *Close-up of another face shifting across a gap.*

750. *Resume on* K. *Sounds of whispering off.*

751. *Another eye, in close-up.*

752. *Resume on* K. *He looks to the right.*

753. *Slight pan to the right across another eye, in close-up.*

TITORELLI *off* : Out! Every . . .

754. *Resume on* K, *looking increasingly nervous.*

TITORELLI *off* : . . . bloody one of you out . . .

755. *Resume on the eye.*

TITORELLI *off* : . . . of my . . .

756. *Resume on* K.

TITORELLI *off* : . . . studio!

757. *Resume on the eye. It disappears, to be replaced by its twin.*

TITORELLI *off* : I really . . .

758. *Close-up of another face in shadow and whip pan left to another, laughing. (Still on page 115)*

TITORELLI : I really must apologise . . .

759. *Medium long shot of* TITORELLI. *Camera pans left as he ejects two more children.*

TITORELLI : . . . for receiving you . . .

760. *Rapid close-up of* K *turning to watch.*

761. *Medium close-up of* TITORELLI *ejecting a child towards camera.*

TITORELLI : . . . like this.

762. *High angle close-up of two grinning faces in shadow, between the slats.*

TITORELLI *off* : Out!

763. *Jump cut to high angle medium shot of* TITORELLI *hurrying to the door with a canvas. More screams.*

764. *Whip pan to and fro, coming to rest on two more faces.*

TITORELLI *off* : Out!

> *765. Low angle medium long shot of* TITORELLI *blocking the door with a framed canvas and turning towards* K, *who stands watching on the right.*

TITORELLI : I got back late last night. That's why everything's in such a mess.

> *The canvas falls down, pushed by a child through one of the gaps.* TITORELLI *turns and picks it up again as he continues, while K picks up an overturned chair.*

TITORELLI : And just as I was tucking myself under the covers a dreadful little . . .

> *766. Low angle medium shot of* K, TITORELLI *in back view in the foreground.*

TITORELLI *continuing* : . . . claw reaches up and seizes me. *He turns towards camera.* She was there under the bed of course, waiting.

> *767. Close-up of two faces looking through the planks.*

A VOICE : Titorelli! . . . Can we come in now?

> *768. Close-up of another grinning face.*

> *769. Low angle long shot,* K *in the background.* TITORELLI *comes towards camera and bends down to address a child through the wall.*

TITORELLI : No you can't!

> *770. Close-up of two more faces.*

ANOTHER VOICE : Not even me?

> *771. Resume on* TITORELLI *(as 769). He moves to another gap in the wall.*

TITORELLI : No! I have some pretty little pussy cats who aren't going to be so pretty when Titorelli's through with them! I have some . . .

> *772. Medium close-up of* TITORELLI *from above. Camera pans right as he prowls along a wall.*

TITORELLI : . . . dirty minded little pussies that are going to wish their mums had drowned them in a bucket!

> *773. High angle medium close-up of* TITORELLI *darting forward by the planking.*

TITORELLI : I'll get my ice pick!

> *774. Close-up of a face. The children are now silent.*

TITORELLI *continues off* : Remember my ice pick!

> *775. Resume on the painter as he gets up.*

TITORELLI : And what can I do for you . . .

776. Medium close-up of him leaning affectedly towards K.

TITORELLI : . . . chum?

777. Shot of the two of them, K nearest camera, which tracks backwards as they move.

K : I . . . I . . . I thought . . . you might be able to give me some advice.

TITORELLI : You wouldn't want to be buying one of my pictures.

K *turning round* : Oh cer . . . certainly. You're . . . you're working on a painting now?

Camera pans right as K goes up to a picture, which the painter immediately uncovers. They stand in front of it, in medium close-up, in profile.

TITORELLI : A portrait — not quite finished.

K : Oh! This must be a judge.

TITORELLI : Judges are my speciality. K *takes out a pair of glasses.*

778. High angle medium close-up of K putting on his glasses and examining the picture, TITORELLI behind him.

K *leaning forward* : What . . . wha . . . what does that repre . . . *He turns as something touches him from behind . . .* represent?

779. As TITORELLI replies, cut to close-up of a grinning face behind the planks.

TITORELLI : You can see for yourself . . .

780. Resume on the two of them (as 778).

TITORELLI : Justice.

K : Yes.

781. Medium close-up of K looking at the painting in the foreground.

K : There . . . there's the . . . there's the bandage over the eyes, but aren't those . . . Ouch! *A child bites* K's *hand from behind the planks. He rubs it* . . . aren't those wings there on the heels?

782. Close-up of TITORELLI. (Still on page 115)

TITORELLI : My instructions were to paint it that way.

783. Resume on K.

K : Flying? Justice ought to stand still, don't you think? Or else the scales are wavering. A just verdict won't be possible. *He looks behind him again.*

TITORELLI *off* : Well actually it's Justice and the goddess of Victory combined.

784. Resume on TITORELLI.

TITORELLI : What does she look like to you ?

785. Close-up of K.

K : Like the Goddess of the Hunt . . . in full cry.

786. Close-up of a child behind the planks. Loud fast jazz again.

A GIRL : Titorelli !

787. Resume on K. *He looks down at the children.*

788. Close-up of another child.

GIRL : Can we come in now !

789. High angle medium shot of TITORELLI. *Camera pans as he rushes angrily across the room.*

TITORELLI : Nasty thing, we're busy !

790. Close-up of another child, and pan to two more behind the slats.

GIRL : You aren't really busy.

791. Close-up of the girl behind the planks.

GIRL *jeering* : You're gonna paint him ? Please don't paint him !

792. Resume on high angle medium shot of TITORELLI. *Camera pans right again as he comes back towards* K *and, in passing, picks up a paintbrush which he wipes on his pyjama jacket.*

GIRL *off* : Not an ugly one like that ! *She giggles.*

TITORELLI *in an undertone* : These girls belong to the court.

K *in a whisper* : Them too, eh ?

TITORELLI : Practically everything belongs to the court. *He moves towards* K. *Camera tilts up to show the two of them in low angle medium close-up.* But it's behind the scenes . . .

793. Low angle close-up of two children. The painter continues off.

TITORELLI : . . . here in this very studio . . .

794. High angle close-up of two more children.

TITORELLI *off* : . . . that's where you get your results.

K *off* : Oh ?

795. Close-up of another child making faces behind the planking.

TITORELLI *off* : I forgot to ask you what kind of acquittal you want.

796. Close-up of two more children.

TITORELLI : Ostensible or . . .

797. Resume on the two men in low angle medium close-up.

TITORELLI : ... definite acquittal or deferment?

798. Two more faces.

TITORELLI *off* : Definite acquittal is the best ...

799. Another girl's face.

TITORELLI *off* : ... but I can't influence ...

800. Another girl. Camera pans as she moves along behind the planking.

TITORELLI *off* : ... that kind of verdict. Nobody can.

801. Resume on medium close-up of the two of them. Camera pans as K passes in front of TITORELLI and walks to the other end of the studio.

K : Oh?

TITORELLI *turning to watch him* : I never in my life heard of a case of definite acquittal. What's wrong?

K *in stifled tones* : Is there ... a window or something we could open?

TITORELLI : Oh well ...

802. Close-up of the children jeering behind the planks.

TITORELLI : ... there's plenty of air comes in ...

803. Resume on the painter in medium close-up from the back. Camera tilts up as he moves towards K.

TITORELLI : ... through those chinks. But if you want some ventilation, you've that door ... *He indicates a door over the bed.*

804. Medium close-up of the two of them from above. K turns.

TITORELLI : ... just behind you. The judge I'm painting ...

805. Close-up of an eye.

TITORELLI *off* : ... now, for instance.

806. Low angle medium close-up of TITORELLI. As he continues, K starts to take off his jacket behind him.

TITORELLI : ... he always comes in by that door, I've had to give him a key for it in case I happen to be out. His Honour usually arrives very early when I'm still asleep. It's not exactly a soothing experience you know, to wake up in the morning and find a judge ... *Noise of the children, off.*

807. High angle reverse shot of the two of them, K taking off his jacket, in back view in the foreground.

TITORELLI : ... all dressed up in those crazy ceremonial robes climbing over your bed.

A GIRL *off* : He's taken off his jacket! *The painter turns round.*

808. Close-up of two children.

TITORELLI *off* : They seem to think . . .

809. Low angle medium close-up of the painter, K in the background. (as 806).

TITORELLI : . . . I'm going to paint your portrait, and that's why you've taken off your jacket.

K : What are the . . . other alternatives?

810. High angle reverse shot (as 807).

TITORELLI : Ah! You mean the legal alternatives?

K : Yes.

TITORELLI *rather petulantly* : I told you : Ostensible . . .

811. Low angle close-up of K, his head lolling, eyes half closed. He mutters the words after the painter.

TITORELLI : . . . acquittal or indefinite deferment.

K *muttering* : Ostensible . . . deferment.

TITORELLI : What's wrong Joey? Aren't you feeling well?

Camera pans right, following K from below, as he moves unsteadily across the studio, eyes closed, his face bathed in sweat.

K *muttering* : No.

812. Close-up of a child's eyes.

813. Resume on K from below, reeling back.

K *weakly* : It must . . . must . . . must be . . . the heat.

814. Low angle shot: TITORELLI sitting in the foreground. K, with his jacket still half off, sits on the bed, exhausted.

TITORELLI *looking round* : If I opened . . .

815. Close-up of children's faces.

TITORELLI *off* : . . . that door — we'll have those girls in here . . .

816. Another similar close-up.

TITORELLI *off* : . . . all over us.

K *off* : Oh don't do that.

817. Resume on the two men (as 814). The painter moves his chair towards K.

TITORELLI : Well now, with ostensible . . .

818. High angle medium close-up of TITORELLI settling himself on his chair, the back of K's head in the foreground.

TITORELLI : . . . acquittal, I write out an affidavit of your innocence . . .

819. Low angle medium close-up of K. *He nods as the painter continues, off.*

TITORELLI *off* : . . . and make the rounds of all the judges I know personally, beginning with the one I'm painting now. I explain to him that you're innocent . . .

820. Resume on the painter from above (as 818).

TITORELLI : . . . and myself guarantee that innocence.

K : And . . .

821. Close-up of K's *face.*

K : . . . if he believes you?

TITORELLI *off* : . . . As he very well might . . . You know we mustn't be too pessimistic — some of them are bound to believe me . . .

K *almost in a whisper* : Yes . . . and I'd be . . .

822. A high shot of the painter (as 820).

K : . . . free.

TITORELLI *getting up* : Ostensibly . . .

823. Medium close-up of the two men, slightly from below, TITORELLI *three-quarters facing camera,* K *in three-quarter back view.*

TITORELLI : Ostensibly free. Naturally the judges I know all belong to the lowest grade. They haven't the power reserved to the highest . . .

824. Close-up of K.

TITORELLI *off* : . . . court of all, to grant a final acquittal.

K : The highest . . . court.

TITORELLI : Chum, that . . .

825. Close-up of children laughing.

TITORELLI *off* : . . . court is inaccessible to you, to me, to all of us.

826. Resume on the two of them (as 823).

TITORELLI : What the prospects are up there, well . . . we just don't know . . . and we don't want to know.

827. Close-up of K's *face.*

TITORELLI *off* : I'm sure you understand.

K : No I'm not sure that I do.

828. Camera pans left with a child's face in close-up.

TITORELLLI *off* : What they can do for you is to . . .

829. Low angle medium close-up of the two men as the painter goes and sits on the bed beside K.

Titorelli : . . . relieve you of the . . .

830. High angle medium close-up of the two of them sitting on the bed, K *nearest camera.*

Titorelli : . . . burden of the charge — lift it from your shoulders for a time . . . But it does hover around up there, above you. You see, in definite acquittal, all the documents are annulled; but with ostensible acquittal, your whole dossier continues to circulate. Up to the higher courts . . .

831. Close-up of the children's faces.

Titorelli *off* : . . . down to the lower ones . . .

832. Close-up of another face looking through the planks.

Titorelli *off* : . . . up again, down, these oscillations . . .

833. Another similar shot.

Titorelli *off* : . . . and peregrinations . . .

834. Low angle close-up of K.

Titorelli *off* : . . . you just can't figure 'em.

K *with a dazed look* : No use trying either, I suppose.

835. High angle close-up of Titorelli *looking off at* K.

836. Resume on K. *He laughs.*

Titorelli *off* : Not a hope.

837. Close-up of the children laughing.

Titorelli *off* : Why, I've known cases . . .

838. Another similar shot.

Titorelli *off* : . . . of an acquitted man coming home from the court . . .

839. Low angle medium shot of him and K *sitting on the bed.*

Titorelli : . . . and finding the cops waiting there to arrest him, all over again . . . But then of course . . .

840. Close-up of a child's face.

Titorelli *off* : . . . theoretically . . .

841. Close-up of an eye. It shifts and is replaced by its twin.

Titorelli *off* : . . . it's always possible to get another ostensible acquittal.

842. Close-up of K.

K : The second acquittal wouldn't be final either.

843. Close-up of Titorelli.

Titorelli : It's automatically followed by the third arrest; the third acquittal by the fourth arrest; the fourth . . .

844. Medium close-up of the two of them, slightly from above.

158

K : And so on.

TITORELLI : You think a deferment . . .

845. *Close-up of a child's face behind the planks.*

TITORELLI : . . . would suit you any better Joey?

846. *Another similar shot.*

K *off* : Well, I . . .

847. *Close-up of* K.

K *hopelessly* : . . . couldn't really say.

TITORELLI *off* : Even then you can't withold a case forever.

848. *Close-up of eyes shifting behind the planks.*

849. *Medium close-up of the two men from below.* K *gets up and, putting on his jacket, goes off. The painter sits up.*

TITORELLI : Measures have to be taken . . .

850. *Close-up. Camera pans right, following the movements of one of the children behind the planks.*

TITORELLI *off* : . . . questions, interrogations, observations . . .

851. *A medium close-up of* K. *Camera tracks forward as he backs away along the wall.*

TITORELLI *off* : . . . more interrogations, evidence collected . . .

852. *Low angle close-up of* TITORELLI *sitting on the bed.*

TITORELLI : Going already?

853. *Close-up of* K *by the door.*

K : I'll be . . . I'll be back to see you again . . . very soon.

854. *Close-up of children's faces from above.*

TITORELLI *off* : I'm going to keep you to your word you know Joey . . .

855. *Another similar shot.*

TITORELLI *off* : . . . otherwise . . .

856. *Close-up of the painter from below.*

TITORELLI : . . . I'll have to call in at your office, and I know you wouldn't . . .

857. *Close-up of* K *by the door.*

TITORELLI *off* : . . . like that.

K *desperately* : Unlock this door will you?

858. *Close-up of a face.*

TITORELLI *off* : You don't want to be bothered . . .

859. *Medium shot of the two men,* K *facing camera,* TITORELLI *in back view in the foreground.*

TITORELLI : . . . by the girls.

860. *Close-up of* K. *He shakes his head weakly.*

861. *Close-up of the painter who leans forward and takes* K *by the hand, drawing him into frame.*

TITORELLI : We'd better slip you out this other way.

862. *Close-up of a grinning face.*

863. *Two more grinning faces.*

TITORELLI *off* : Now wait! Wait!

K *off* : What for?

864. *Low angle medium shot of the painter as he crawls under the bed while* K *climbs on top of it to reach the other door. Camera tilts up with* K.

TITORELLI : Wouldn't you like to see some of my pictures?

Camera tilts down again to show TITORELLI *tossing canvasses out from under the bed.*

TITORELLI : I'm sure there's at least one or two of them . . .

865. *High angle medium close-up of a painting landing on the floor.*

TITORELLI *off* : . . . you'd want to buy.

866. *Close-up of a girl peering through the planks.*

867. *Close-up of two girls laughing. Sound of their laughter.*

TITORELLI *off* : What about this?

868. *Medium shot of the two of them. The painter shows* K *a picture as he stands on the bed.*

TITORELLI : This one . . . it's modern you know. An action painting. I call it 'Wild Nature'.

869. *Medium close-up of* K. *He glances at the picture and takes hold of it.*

K : Okay, I'll buy it.

870. *Resume on medium shot. The painter seizes another picture and shows it to him. Music.*

TITORELLI : Here's the companion picture.

871. *Resume on medium close-up of* K, *glancing at the picture and taking it even more abruptly than before.*

K : I'll take them both. *He turns to go.*

TITORELLI *off* : You seem to like the subject.

K : Yes I do. I . . . I . . .

TITORELLI *off* : Hmmm.

K : I'll hang them in my office.

TITORELLI *off* : Now by a lucky chance . . .

872. *Resume on medium shot of the two of them.*

TITORELLI *holding up another picture* : ... I've got another ...

873. *Medium close-up of* K, *already encumbered by his two pictures. A third appears on left of frame as* TITORELLI *offers it to him.*

TITORELLI *off* : ... on the very same theme.

K : How ... how much are the three?

874. *Resume on medium shot of both.*

TITORELLI : Oh, we'll settle that the next time. Today you're in such a hurry.

Camera tracks in on them as the painter gets up onto the bed and K *backs out through the door.*

TITORELLI : But we're going to keep in real close touch with each other from now on, aren't we Joey boy?

875. *A closer shot of* K *as he backs out through the door and turns, astonished, as he finds himself in the corridor full of files and archives, inside the court building. The painter watches, partly visible in the foreground. Music.*

876. *Long shot of the corridor with its palely lit ceiling and rows of filing systems on either side.*

877. *Medium close-up of* K : *he turns in astonishment to the painter, who is standing in the doorway behind him.*

878. *Reverse angle medium shot of* K *through the doorway,* TITORELLI *leaning across it in the foreground. (Still on page 116)*

K *in amazement* : This is the law court office.

TITORELLI : That seems to surprise you.

879. *Reverse shot (as 877).* K *moves forward.*

880. *Medium shot of* K *(as 878). He walks off down the corridor, watched by* TITORELLI *who is partly visible in the foreground.*

K : I think what surprises me most is how ignorant I am about everything concerning this court of yours. *He turns to face the painter.* For an accused man ...

881. *Medium close-up of* TITORELLI *peering through the doorway.*

K *off* : ... that's a mistake.

882. *Long shot of the corridor, tilted down to the left.* K *stands in medium shot, clutching his painting, facing* TITORELLI

off-screen.

K : He should never let himself be caught napping — never for a moment let his eyes . . .

883. A closer shot of TITORELLI.

K *off* : . . . stray to the left . . .

884. Resume on K.

K : . . . when, for all he knows, a judge or somebody like that might be lurking a little bit to the right. *He starts to back away down the corridor.* Oh!

885. Long shot of a group of men, the accused, sitting against a wall in front of a filing system. They get up as K *approaches off-screen.*

K *off* : You!

886. Reverse angle medium shot of K. *He takes a step forward.*

K *laughing ironically* : I make you very uncomfortable don't I? It distresses you to find me in your company.

887. Resume on the men. They stare uneasily.

K *off* : Yes I've been told all about that.

888. Resume on K.

K *with mounting hysteria* : Before I thought you . . . you took me for a judge or at least an official of the court. I even thought you were afraid of me, but what you're feeling is pain!

889. Long shot of the men. They move back in silence.

K *off* : You don't like what you see do you?

890. Resume on K.

K *pointing at his mouth and laughing hysterically* : It's my mouth! *(Still on page 116)* You think you can tell from my mouth that I'm condemned! That I'm going to be . . .

891. Reverse angle medium long shot of K *seen in back view through the doorway. He throws down the pictures.*

K : . . . found guilty! . . . Guilty!

892. Resume on the men who all move forward slightly.

893. Resume on K *from behind. He backs through the door into a corridor, made from wooden slats like the painter's studio.*

894. Close-up of the children, jeering at him through the planking. The camera pans to and fro across their faces.

895. Resume on K *in medium shot. Track backwards as he runs down the corridor towards us. Loud music. The children follow him on the outside with bloodthirsty cries.*

896. Low angle close-up of K running, streaked with the light coming through the slats.

897. Another similar shot. Camera pans from left to right, following K from below.

898. Pan to hold on close-up of a child's face, teeth bared.

899. Resume on backward tracking shot of K running.

900. Rapid panning shot across the wooden slats.

901. Camera tracks in on the children advancing, seen through the slats.

902. Long shot of the corridor. (Still on page 149) At the other end K goes out of frame, followed by his shadow.

903. In the next shot we are in a long, sewer-like underground passage. K's shadow looms on the vaulted ceiling as he arrives panting, seen from below. (Still on page 149)

904. Backward tracking shot of K running, seen from below.

905. A similar tracking shot: K seen in close-up from below. Children's screams off. He looks ahead in alarm.

906. Long shot down the passage. The children appear in the distance.

907. Medium close-up of K, who sees them, turns and dashes off in the opposite direction.

908. Long shot of the children chasing after K down the tunnel, camera tracking out in front of them.

909. Similar shot of K, looking back nervously as he runs.

910. Closer backward tracking shot of the children, seen from below. Their screaming continues.

911. Long shot of the children from below, pursuing K, who is seen in the distance.

912. Resume on backward tracking shot of K seen in medium close-up from below. He stumbles but keeps going.

913. Backward tracking shot of the approaching children, seen in medium close-up.

914. Medium shot of K running, pursued by the children. He pauses and looks back.

915. Low angle medium shot of the children hurtling down the passage, still screaming.

916. Another shot of K running. Pan left to right as he passes camera.

917. *Long shot of the passing children from behind.*

918. *Medium shot of* K. *He leaps down a step, going away from camera.*

919. *Reverse angle medium close-up of* K *as he jumps down the step and arrives at an intersection in the passage, lit by an electric bulb. He looks back nervously, goes round a pillar and off to the right, then comes back, goes round the pillar again and off to the left. Camera pans to follow him as he dodges to and fro, then tracks out in front of him from below, as he runs off down a new passage. He sees the children still coming after him along an overhead gallery which connects with the passage by a series of skylights. The girls' shouts begin to sound like the cries of animals but they remain in the gallery overhead.*

920. *Similar tracking shot of the children, seen from below through the skylights. The track continues into blackness. The noise dies away.*

921. *Camera continues the same movement, tracking and panning across a series of stained-glass windows.*

922. *Dissolve to interior shot of a cathedral, in semi-darkness. We see* K *in long shot from above, coming to a halt near a large pillar. A deep voice rings out.*

VOICE : Joseph K! Joseph K!

K looks round for the source of the voice. Camera tracks in and cranes down towards him as he walks past the pillar, then pans right and tilts up as he advances towards an imposing pulpit. A PRIEST *leans over the edge towards him. We see the two of them from below:* K *in the foreground looking up at the* PRIEST. *(Still on page 150)*

PRIEST : You are Joseph K?

K : Yes.

PRIEST : An accused man?

K : So I've been informed.

PRIEST : Your case is going badly.

A pause.

K : My first petition hasn't been offered yet.

PRIEST : For the present, your guilt is assumed to have been proved.

K : But I'm not guilty.

The PRIEST *turns and comes down from the pulpit. Camera*

pans right and tilts down to follow K *as he goes to meet him.*
K : For that matter, how can any man be found guilty? We're all simply men here, one as much as the other.
PRIEST : The guilty always talk like that. *A pause.* What do you propose to do now?
K : Get more help. *He walks away.*
PRIEST : Help?
> *Camera pans right, cutting out the* PRIEST, *and tracks after* K *as he walks towards a large black curtain, probably the exit.*
K : There are several possibilities I haven't explored yet.
PRIEST *off* : You expect too much from outside help, especially from women.
> K *turns and retraces his steps. Camera pans left to show the two of them,* K *with his back to camera, the* PRIEST *facing him several yards away.*
K : Women have influence. Take that examining magistrate. He has only to see a woman and he'll climb over the bench and knock down the defendant just to get his hands on her. *Pan right as he makes for the exit again.* Yeah, that's an aspect of the court you probably don't know much about. *Pushing aside the curtain, he goes out, only to find himself in darkness.*
> *923. A closer shot of the curtain itself.*
K *continues off* : Where's the door? I've got to catch up with my work at the office.
> *924. Close-up of* K *from behind, in the darkness. Camera tracks right with him as he gropes for the way out.*
K : After all I'm the assistant manager of my department.
A VOICE *off whispers* : Joseph! *He turns.*
> *925. Medium shot of the* ADVOCATE *coming slowly forwards from behind a pillar.*
K *off* : What are you doing in church?
> *926. Reverse shot,* K *in the background, facing the* ADVOCATE, *who is in back view in the foreground. (Still on page 150)*
K *stepping forward* : . . . Or am I still in church? Or is this part of the law court offices.
> *927. As* K *finishes, off, cut to low angle medium close-up of the* ADVOCATE *walking towards him.*
ADVOCATE : I left my sick bed.
> *928. Low angle medium close-up of* K, *silhouetted against a*

165

strong light.

K : Well go back to your sick bed. *He turns and moves away and the light shines directly at the camera, filling the screen.*

ADVOCATE *off* : Joseph you don't seriously believe . . .

    929. Camera tilts up to low angle medium close-up of the ADVOCATE.

ADVOCATE : . . . you can defend yourself? *He steps forward.*

    930. Low angle medium close-up of K. *Camera tracks with him as he walks towards the source of the light.*

K : Big choice! Defend myself or defy you!

ADVOCATE *off* : Defy the court?

K : All of you . . . What's this? *He arrives at the source of light—a slide projector standing on a table.*

    931. Close-up of the ADVOCATE *in shadow.*

ADVOCATE : We use these . . .

    932. Close-up of K, *the* ADVOCATE *in shadow behind him.*

ADVOCATE : . . . visual aids . . .

K *angrily* : Lectures and sermons! *He strides forward, out of frame.*

ADVOCATE : Yes.

    933. Medium close-up of K *standing, brilliantly lit by the ray of light from the slide projector, which throws his shadow on the empty screen behind him. (Still on page 150) As he speaks off-screen, the* ADVOCATE *moves the slide across in front of the lens and one of the pin-head images of the fortress gate, seen at the beginning of the film, appears on the screen behind* K. *He turns to look at it.*

ADVOCATE *off* : Now your particular delusions . . .

    934. Close-up of him standing by the projector.

ADVOCATE : . . . are described in the writings . . .

    935. Resume on the picture.

ADVOCATE *off* : . . . which preface the Law. K *himself is off-screen. His shadow moves as he walks towards the picture. The* ADVOCATE *continues.* Before the Law there stands a Guard. A Man comes from the country, seeking admittance to the Law. *The slide changes to show the* GUARD *and the* MAN *standing by the gate.* But the Guard cannot admit him. K's *shadow moves to the right.* Can the Man hope to enter at a later time?

K *petulantly* : I've heard it all before. We've all heard it. *His shadow moves as he turns towards the projector off-screen. The*

Man is dying of old age, still waiting there, and just at the end the Guard tells him that the door was meant for him, only for him.

936. Medium shot of the ADVOCATE *standing by the projector, holding one of the slides.*

ADVOCATE : The Guard tells him no-one could enter this door.

937. Low angle medium close-up of K *himself, silhouetted against the picture, his shadow behind him. (Still on page 150)*

ADVOCATE *off, in a whisper* : And now . . .

938. Close-up of the ADVOCATE'S *face.*

ADVOCATE : . . . I'm going to close it.

939. Close-up of the projector as he changes the picture.

940. Resume on the screen. K *moves nervously as the picture changes to show the door shut.*

ADVOCATE *off* : Some commentators . . .

941. Low angle medium close-up of K, *standing in front of the image of the doorway. The* ADVOCATE'S *shadow is now visible on the left of the picture.*

ADVOCATE *off* : . . . have pointed out that the Man came to the door . . .

942. Close-up of the ADVOCATE.

ADVOCATE : . . . of his own free will.

K : And we're supposed to swallow all that?

943. Resume on K *(as 941).*

K : It's all true?

ADVOCATE : We needn't accept everything as true.

944. Close-up of him.

ADVOCATE : Only what's necessary.

945. Close-up of K, *half in shadow, in front of the screen.*

K : God, what a miserable conclusion! It turns lying into a universal principle. *He moves away angrily.*

946. Medium shot of the screen. We now see the shadows of both men on the picture. K's *shadow crosses that of the* ADVOCATE *and goes out of frame to the left.*

ADVOCATE : You're attempting to defy the court. By such an obviously mad gesture you hope to . . .

947. Reverse angle medium shot of the two men. The ADVOCATE *turns round as* K *goes towards the projector.*

ADVOCATE : . . . plead insanity. You've laid some foundation to that claim by appearing to believe yourself the victim . . .

948. Resume on the screen. The picture is changed, obviously by K. *The image of the gateway disappears and the* ADVOCATE's *shadow is projected on the blank screen.*

ADVOCATE *off* : . . . of some kind of conspiracy.

K *off* : That's a symptom of lunacy . . .

949. Resume on K *standing beside the projector. The* ADVOCATE *is partly visible in the foreground, his back to camera.*

K : . . . isn't it? *Camera tracks in as he comes towards the* ADVOCATE.

ADVOCATE : Delusions of persecution.

950. Medium close-up of the two of them standing face to face in front of the screen. (Still on page 150)

K : Delusions?

ADVOCATE : Well?

K : I don't pretend . . .

951. Reverse shot (as 949).

K : . . . to be a martyr. No. *He moves out of frame.*
The ADVOCATE, *in close-up, follows him with his eyes.*

ADVOCATE : Not even a victim of society?

952. Medium long shot of K *standing by himself in front of the blank screen.*

K : I am a member of society.

ADVOCATE *off* : You think you can persuade the court that you're not responsible by reason of lunacy?

K : I think that's what the court wants me to believe. *A pause.* Yes, that's the conspiracy.

953. Medium close-up of the ADVOCATE *coming forward.*

K *continues off* : . . . to persuade us all that the whole world's crazy . . .

954. Resume on K.

K : Formless, meaningless, . . .

955. Resume on the ADVOCATE.

K *off* : . . . absurd. That's the dirty game.

956. Resume on K.

K : So I've lost my case. What of it? You . . . you're losing too.
The light on the screen goes out.

957. Close-up of K.

K : It's all . . .

168

958. Close-up of the ADVOCATE.

K *off* : ... lost. Lost!

959. Resume on K. Music.

K : So what? Does that sentence the entire universe to lunacy? *He turns to go.*

960. Close-up of the ADVOCATE *watching him.*

961. Low angle medium shot of K. Camera tracks after him as he looks for the exit.

962. Low angle medium close-up of the PRIEST *coming forward. Camera tilts up slightly.*

PRIEST : Can't you see anything at all?

963. Resume on K. Camera tracks and pans as he makes for the door.

K : Of course, I'm responsible.

PRIEST *coming forward on the right* : My son.

K *turns round and pauses in the doorway.*

964. Close-up of K.

K : I'm not your son. *He turns and goes out.*

965. Low angle long shot of K as he comes out of the cathedral. Camera cranes up and tilts down simultaneously as he walks across the precinct.

966. High angle long shot of K coming towards camera, which tilts slowly down as he advances. (Still on page 151) We hear the noise of his footsteps. He halts and looks up.

967. Low angle reverse shot. Standing in back view in the foreground, K sees two policemen in plain clothes, who seem to be waiting for him, at the top of a short flight of steps. (Still on page 151) The two policemen come down the steps, intercept K and, silently, each takes hold of one of his arms. They lead him away. Throughout the following sequence, a viola plays softly off.

968. Low angle long shot of the cathedral precinct. The trio come towards camera and off to the left, seen from ground level.

969. High angle long shot of the three of them walking along a dimly lit street.

970. A closer, high angle shot. They come round a corner and walk away from camera. K struggles intermittently. (Still on

169

971. Long shot as they walk off into the distance.

972. Low angle long shot of them descending a sloping street, almost running. (Still on page 151)

973. Shot of the three of them from behind, crossing an open space in front of two large modern buildings.

974. Medium shot of the three of them from below, passing between the pillars at the base of one of the buildings. The camera tracks backwards in front of them.

975. Long shot of a piece of waste ground at night. Camera pans left to follow the three men as they pass behind a row of concrete drain-pipes. (Still on page 151)

976. High angle long shot: camera pans briefly left as they hurry down a bank at the side of a road, between some shacks.

977. Another long shot: camera pans left as they walk along a street, lined with dilapidated houses.

978. Long shot of the open space where the shrouded statue stands, a row of street lamps behind. The trio cross frame from right to left.

979. Low angle medium shot: they come down a bank, towards camera.

980. High angle reverse shot: they hurry down and along a river bank, lined with leafless trees. Dawn is gradually breaking. [¹*At one point K stops, forcing his companions to do likewise. They seem like two nurses guarding a sick man, waiting for him to recover his breath. After a moment K tries to struggle.*

K : Why should I follow you?

The struggle continues in silence. Then K sees something in the distance. Something unexpected and unhoped for.

K : Miss Burstner! . . . Miss Burstner! . . . Marika! . . .

She is some way away. K rushes after her with the two men still hanging onto his arms.

K *shouting* : Will I never be able to reach her?

They go faster, looking almost like three dancers linked together.

K : At least we could look at her. She seems to be limping . . . Perhaps it's someone else. I thought I recognised her coat. But no

---

¹ The following scene occurs in Welles's original script, but was not shot.

doubt it's her friend . . . Or her sister? . . . What was she called?
Miss Pittl. Perhaps she gave her her coat . . . What's the matter?
She turns down a small side street. What's the matter?

After a pause he starts to run again. The two men are out of breath as if they have had to chase him.]

981. *Another shot of the three of them hurrying away from camera, silhouetted against the horizon. They halt as they finally arrive at a small stony pit, abandoned and desolate. The viola music continues.*

982. *A closer shot of the same scene. The policemen release* K, *although one of them tries to seize hold of his jacket.* K *reacts violently. Then, calming down, he starts to take off his jacket while one of the policemen motions him to step back. The* POLICEMAN *pushes him. He falls down into the pit.*

983. *We see* K *in medium shot from above as he lands in the stony pit and falls over.*

984. *Medium close-up of* K *getting to his feet and gazing upwards. Camera tilts up and pans slightly right.*

985. *Medium long shot of the policemen from below, walking round the edge of the pit. Camera pans right with them.*

986. *Resume on* K *from above looking up at them. After a pause he finally takes off his jacket and puts it down on a piece of stone, then starts to take off his tie, looking anxiously up at the policemen as he does so.*

987. *Resume on the two policemen, shot from below, watching him in silence. Sound of cicadas.*

988. *A high shot of* K *as he takes off his waistcoat.*

989. *Resume on the policemen watching.*

990. *Resume on* K. *He takes off his shirt, still looking up at them.*

991. *Another shot of the policemen from below.*

992. *Resume on* K. *He bundles up his shirt and starts to put it down.*

993. *High angle medium shot of* K *putting his shirt down on the stone, on top of his waistcoat and jacket.*

994. *Resume on the policemen. They move off left. The music fades out.*

995. *Resume on* K. *He sits down on a stone.*

996. *Medium shot of the policemen from below, scrambling*

down the side of the pit towards K. *Camera pans right with them.*

997. Reverse shot from above as the policemen arrive at the bottom and stand over K. *They look at him in silence. Then one of them bends down, picks up* K's *jacket, rolls it up and puts it on the ground behind him.*

998. Medium close-up of the three of them. One of the policemen takes hold of K's *head and lays it back on the jacket. (Still on page 152) He and his colleague sit down, with* K *lying on the ground between them. The following scene takes place in silence except for the sound of the cicadas.*

999. Rapid close-up of the two of them sitting down.

1000. Low angle close-up of one of the policemen, as seen by K.

1001. Similar close-up of the SECOND POLICEMAN, *with thick-lensed glasses.*

1002. High angle close-up of K *as seen by them.*

1003. Low angle close-up of the FIRST POLICEMAN *producing a long leather case.*

1004. Close-up of the SECOND POLICEMAN *watching him.*

1005. Close-up of K *from above.*

1006. Resume on the FIRST POLICEMAN *who hands the case to his colleague.*

1007. Resume on K *watching.*

1008. Medium close-up of the SECOND POLICEMAN *as he takes the case and removes from it a butcher's knife which he turns in his fingers, inspecting it. (Still on page 152)*

1009. Close-up of K, *looking very alarmed.*

1010. Medium shot of the three of them from above as the SECOND POLICEMAN *hands back the knife to his colleague, who bends over* K *as he takes it.*

1011. Close-up of the knife passing very close to K's *face.*

1012. Low angle medium close-up of the FIRST POLICEMAN *taking back the knife. (Still on page 152)*

1013. Resume on K, *the knife-blade just disappearing on the left of frame.*

1014. Close-up of the FIRST POLICEMAN. *He hands the knife across again.*

1015. Close-up of the SECOND POLICEMAN *leaning forward*

to take the knife.

1016. Close-up of the knife being passed over K's *face.*

1017. High angle medium shot of the three of them: the SECOND POLICEMAN *takes the knife.*

1018. Low angle close-up of the SECOND POLICEMAN. *He fingers the knife again.*

1019. Low angle medium close-up of the FIRST POLICEMAN *sitting back.*

1020. Close-up of K *from above.*

K : You expect me to take the knife and do the job myself?

1021. Medium close-up of the SECOND POLICEMAN *sitting silently.*

K *off, in a whisper* : No, you'll have to do it.

1022. Low angle close-up of the FIRST POLICEMAN *gazing down at* K. *He looks up at his colleague.*

1023. Resume on the SECOND POLICEMAN. *He gets up.*

1024. A closer shot of him getting up, holding the knife.

1025. Low angle close-up of the FIRST POLICEMAN *getting up. He looks down as* K *speaks off.*

K : You!

1026. Resume on K *looking up at him. Music.*

1027. Resume on the FIRST POLICEMAN. *He looks at his colleague and jerks his head.*

1028. Medium close-up of the two policemen. The first one moves off left, followed by his colleague.

1029. High angle medium shot of the two men moving away from K. K *starts to get up.*

K *in a hoarse whisper* : You!

1030. Medium close-up of the two policemen. They turn at the sound of his voice.

1031. Medium close-up of K *as he gets up, camera tilting up with him.*

1032. Resume on the two policemen. The FIRST POLICEMAN *takes the knife from his colleague.*

1033. Medium close-up of K *watching them, furious.*

1034. Medium close-up of the two policemen. They turn to go.

1035. Resume on K *watching them.*

K *in a furious whisper* : You!

1036. Resume on the two policemen as they start to climb the sloping side of the pit.

1037. Back to K *watching them, his face black with fury.*

K *yelling at the top of his voice* : You !

1038. The word is long and drawn out and still echoes after the policemen as we see them from below, scrambling away at the top of the pit; camera pans right with them.

1039. Long shot of K *from above. He yells again.*

K : You !

1040. Long shot of the policemen from below. They come back to the top of the bank and look down at K.

K *off* : You . . . hoo . . . !

1041. Resume on K *from above, pointing up at them and yelling.*

K : You dummy !

1042. Another shot of the policemen from below.

K *off* : You'll have to do it.

1043. Low angle medium close-up of K *pointing up at them furiously.*

K : You'll have to kill me !

1044. Resume on the policemen. The First Policeman *puts his hand in his pocket.*

1045. Resume on K. *He waves an arm.*

K *hysterically* : Come on !

1046. Resume on the policemen who produce a stick of dynamite and light a match.

K *off* : Come on !

1047. Long shot of K *from above. He bursts out laughing.*

1048. Long shot of the policemen from below as the fuse ignites.

1049. Low angle medium close-up of K, *laughing hysterically.*

1050. Resume on the policemen. They throw the lighted stick of dynamite into the pit and run off.

1051. Close-up of the dynamite landing near K. *(Still on page 152) He continues to laugh, off.*

1052. Long shot of the waste-ground with the policemen running away from the pit, towards camera. K's *laughter gets more hysterical still.*

1053. Low angle medium close-up of him laughing. (Still on page 152)

1054. High angle medium shot of the two policemen running away.

1055. Close-up of the dynamite from above. The fuse burns down.

1056. Quick long shot of K from above as he bends down to pick something up (a stone? the dynamite?) and starts to throw it.[1]

1057. Medium long shot of the two policemen, seen from behind, crouching down with their faces to the ground.

1058. Long shot of the empty waste-ground. We hear K laughing hysterically off. There is a massive explosion.

1059. Long shot of another explosion.

1060. Another explosion: a column of fire and smoke.

1061. Another explosion.

1062. A fifth explosion.

1063. Camera holds on the sixth and final explosion, tilting up as a column of black smoke rises into the air and billows across the screen. Loud music. The leitmotif of the film — Albinoni's Adagio — *replaces the sound of the explosion. After a while, the music gets softer and we hear the voice of Orson Welles off.*

ORSON WELLES : The film *The Trial* was based on the novel by Franz Kafka.

1064. Dissolve to still shot of another column of smoke, vaguely mushroom-shaped.[2]

ORSON WELLES *off* : The actors in order of their appearance were : Anthony Perkins, Arnoldo Foa, Jess Hahn, William Kearns, Madeleine Robinson, Jeanne Moreau, Maurice Teynac, Maydra Shore, Suzanne Flon, Raoul Delfosse, Jean-Claude Remoleux, Max Buchsbaum, Karl Studer, Max Haufler, Romy Schneider, Fernand Ledoux, Akim Tamiroff, Elsa Martinelli, Thomas Holtzmann, Wolfgang Reichmann, William Chapel and Michael Lonsdale.

1065. Dissolve to a close-up of the front of the slide projector

---

[1] This shot, which lasts less than a second, is highly significant, as in contrast to Kafka's ending, it leaves a glimmer of hope.

[2] Many journalists have suggested that the explosion is intended to be that of an atomic bomb. In fact, close attention to this series of shots and to the soundtrack reveals that it is a series of explosions of dynamite at the most, and that the final cloud of smoke in no way resembles the mushroom-cloud of an atomic explosion.

with one of the pin-head images visible in the lens. There is a dazzle effect from the projector's lamp.

ORSON WELLES *off* : I played the Advocate . . . *The dazzle effect is cut off and the image becomes clearer* . . . and wrote and directed this film. My name is Orson Welles.

1066. Dissolve to the pin-head image projected on the screen. It shows the gate of the fortress, almost shut. Fade out.